PATCHES OF MY LIFE

Youth in the South

KENNETH D. FLY

iUniverse LLC
Bloomington

PATCHES OF MY LIFE
YOUTH IN THE SOUTH

iUniverse books may be ordered through booksellers or by contacting:

iUniverse
1663 Liberty Drive
Bloomington, IN 47403
www.iuniverse.com
1-800-Authors (1-800-288-4677)

ISBN: 978-1-4917-2962-5 (sc)
ISBN: 978-1-4917-2964-9 (hc)
ISBN: 978-1-4917-2963-2 (e)

Library of Congress Control Number: 2014905315

Printed in the United States of America.

iUniverse rev. date: 03/25/2014

CONTENTS

INTRODUCTION

This is a collection of stories about my life on the farm in the South. I wrote these stories in my own words, complete with grammar and spelling errors the computer couldn't figure out how to fix.

If you are interested in knowing what it was like to have a life-changing experience at a young age and grow up on a farm in the late forties, fifties, and sixties, welcome aboard. Although our lifestyle and the means to change it were pretty much fixed, at the time, it was in many ways the same as several other families in the area. We enjoyed a very happy life without much complaining. The struggles were an effort to live happily, make the best of what we had, and try to make the future better.

All of the stories are based on my memories as a boy. These stories are true to the best of my memory and took place between the years of 1941 and 1965. My motivation for this effort was based on the idea that if I didn't write these stories, my children and grandchildren would never know about some of the events that took place during the time of my early years on this earth.

I also needed to point out to the youth that any and all education that can be obtained is a good thing, but higher education is not absolutely necessary to be successful in this great country. Basic education, common sense, and dedication to a goal will get you where you want to be in most cases.

ONE

The Early Years, 1941–1947

In order to set the stage for the lifestyle changes that took place in 1947, I would like to give a little history of the family. The history of any family, I believe, has a lot to do with the mind-set and environment of the children born into that family.

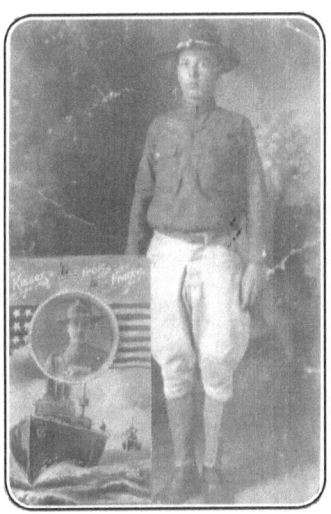

My father, Thomas Jessie Fly, in 1919

My dad was born in 1898 near Rocky Mount, North Carolina, and was a veteran of World War I. He was a victim of mustard gas, causing him lung problems for the rest of his life. If there is such a thing as having too much pride, he was a perfect example. Although he had a certificate of wounded in action, he would not take any assistance from the government as long as he could work and make enough to provide for his family. He fathered ten children, two of which met early deaths due to childhood diseases. The other eight, none of which had physical or mental illness or deformities, finished high school. He was a carpenter and a very religious man who raised a family under strict rules. The cold rough winters, along with health problems, caused Dad to make the decision that would make drastic changes in the lifestyles of the entire family.

Mother was born in the mountains of West Virginia, near Hinton. Mother and Dad both came from large families, and by the time I came along, they had settled in Parkersburg, West Virginia. Mom was a homemaker, and she had a good head on her shoulders about managing assets.

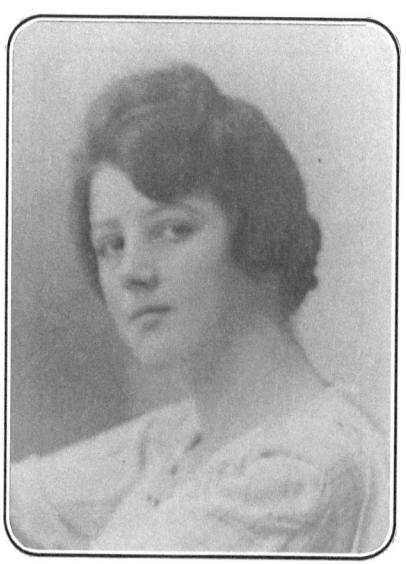

My mother, Glagys Gertha,(Young),Fly in her younger years

On June 7, 1941, I was born as the youngest of eight living children in a house on Putnam Street in Parkersburg.

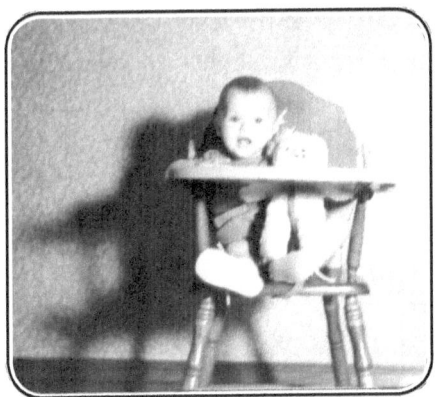

1941 Me as a baby

As history tells us, not long after my birth, World War II broke out and changed the lives of most people in this country. Two brothers-in-law and my oldest brother Edward went to war, along with the rest of the men and women who paid the price for freedom in the United States.

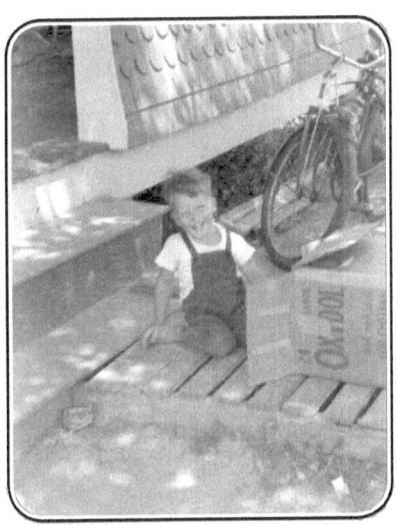

Taken by my brother Edward when he returned home at the end of World War II

My childhood from birth until about five years old is not something I remember a lot about. I do remember, however, the day Ed came home from the navy after the war.

As time has passed, I have written several songs and included the words of two of them in this book: "Dad Was the Head of Our Home" and "Mama Found a Dollar."

TWO

The Old Farmhouse

The first recollection I have of the farm was the old farmhouse. We arrived in the town of Monroe, where we stopped at the only hotel, which was in an old building in the main part of town. We had been on the road for several hours traveling from Parkersburg, West Virginia, through the mountains by the way that was before interstates or even the West Virginia Turnpike. Needless to say, everybody was beat after the two days of travel, but because none of us had seen our new home, we decided to drive out and take a quick look around.

When we arrived, the moving van was there sitting in front of the house. To the older men, it seemed the thing to do would be to unload while they were all there and not wait until morning. It would make sense that the driver would want to head back to West Virginia as soon as he could, so that is what they did. This turned out to be a rather large task with no electricity or running water in the house. The truck driver had a helper, a big black man who was apparently superstitious. He broke a mirror and went on and on about how seven years of bad luck would follow such an action. I can't recall ever seeing him after that so I can't say much about the bad luck it might have caused.

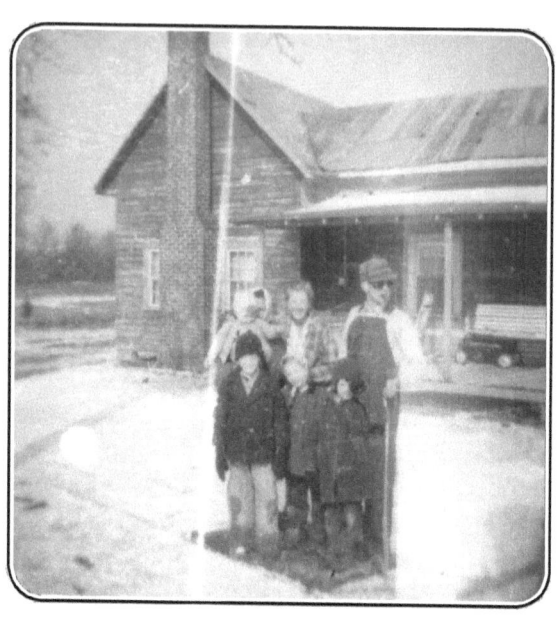

Home in North Carolina with our neighbor family the Hannah's

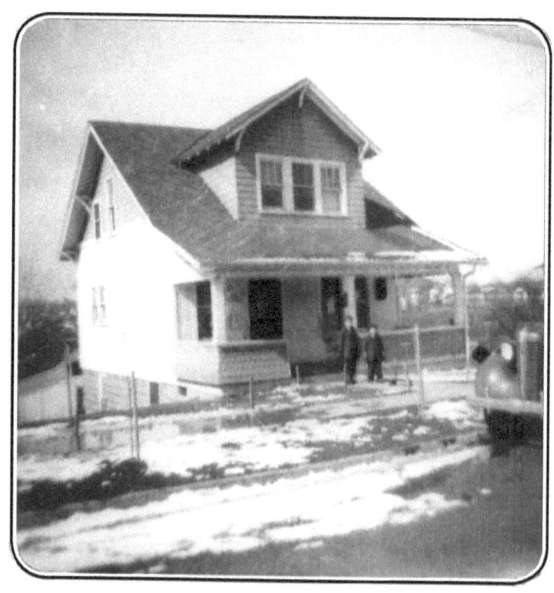

Home in West Virginia, 1942

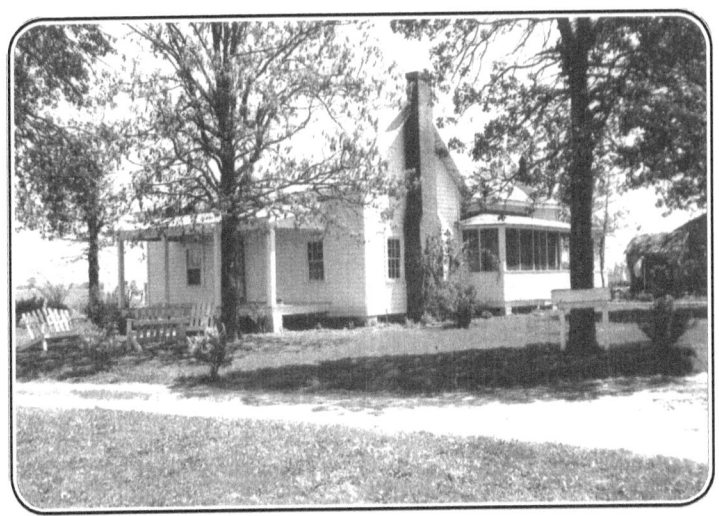

Home in North Carolina with the Hannah
family, who were neighbors, 1947

It is hard to tell you just what we saw . The driveway was not really a driveway. It was more like a yard with no grass that had washed away several times and left ditches in the dirt. The old house was a one-story farmhouse that appeared to have been abandoned for some time. It was covered with unpainted wooden German siding. The house looked more like an old sharecropper's house than anything else. Of course, most of us had never seen anything like it before.

The home we left in Parkersburg was a two-story frame house in good shape with a basement, electricity, natural gas, heat, and running water, and it was in town with paved streets and concrete curbs along the sidewalk. What had we done! At five years of age, I was just along for the ride, but Mom was rather disappointed to say the least. While the men unloaded the moving truck, we sat in the car because it was a cool, rainy night and there was nowhere else to go. It seemed like a long time, but we finally headed to the hotel, which was about five miles from the farm. We spent the night, and everybody was glad to get a bath and a night's sleep.

The next day, we returned to the farm and got our first look in the daylight. I will have to say again that it is hard to put into words what the place looked like. The house was sitting on rock pillars with no underpinning. The yard had no grass, and it was not what you could call a pretty sight. Nevertheless, we were here, and it was going to be our new home. The house was sitting there with some post oak trees around it, two well shelters, a grain building that seemed to be in better shape than the house, and a barn with a hayloft. The road in front was dirt with very little gravel on it. The well covers were there to keep the rain off when drawing water. One was a dug well about twenty-five feet deep, which was mostly surface water, and the other was a drilled well that gave a limited supply of mineral water. It wasn't the best-tasting water around, but it was wet and cold. Neither well had a pump, so all water had to be drawn by hand.

As I said, the house had no underpinning. Neither did it have insulation in the walls or overhead. The floor from the kitchen to the living room had about a ten- to twenty-degree slope, which was good for anything with wheels to coast. To remedy this, Dad and my brother Don went to the woods and cut down a tree. And with an ax, they hewed out a log that would reach from the back wall through the kitchen and dining room, placed it under the house, and leveled the floor with jacks.

Dad was a carpenter and could see the potential of the old house, but not everyone had the same insight or imagination. The floors were made of wood planks with some rather wide cracks between them. We laughed about seeing the chickens under the house without having to go outside, but it was no joke. As Dad fixed the house, he put linoleum on the floor, and when the wind would blow, the floor would raise up two or three inches. Linoleum was like vinyl and came twelve feet wide and cut to the length of a room. The source of heat was a warm morning stove in the living room and a small stove in the kitchen. We had an LP gas cook stove in the kitchen, but bottled gas was rather expensive, so we surely could not use it for heat. Speaking of gas, we also had a gas-operated refrigerator, and as a boy, it was a mystery to me how you could have a fire down below and ice up above. After understanding how refrigeration worked, it was simple, but not for a kid my age.

Living in a cold house was certainly a challenge. We all had so many covers on at night that you could hardly turn over. The window ice was sometimes a quarter-inch thick, and you mostly hoped that you wouldn't have to go to the bathroom in the middle of the night during the winter. When we moved in, we only had a fireplace, and everybody laughed about all the sardine cans that came out of it when we got there.

All things considered, all the drawbacks of the old way of life weren't too bad after all. I will have to admit that remembering it is not near as painful as living it was.

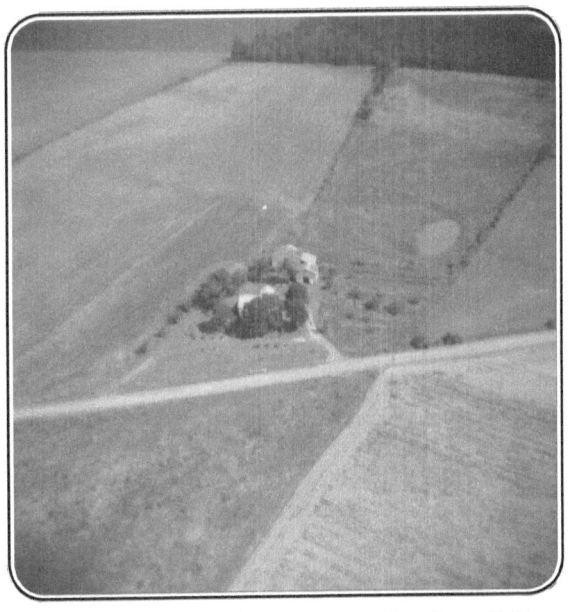

Aerial view of our farm in North Carolina, 1959

THREE

The Cotton Patch

If you have never had to plant, chop, and pick cotton, you have no idea of what can and does happen in the cotton patch. Our main source of machinery was drawn by a horse named Nellie. The next source of energy was family members and hand tools, mainly a hoe and shovel. We were not the only farmers without the needed machinery so we really didn't let it affect us adversely, and we went on to raise a crop the old, slow, hard way.

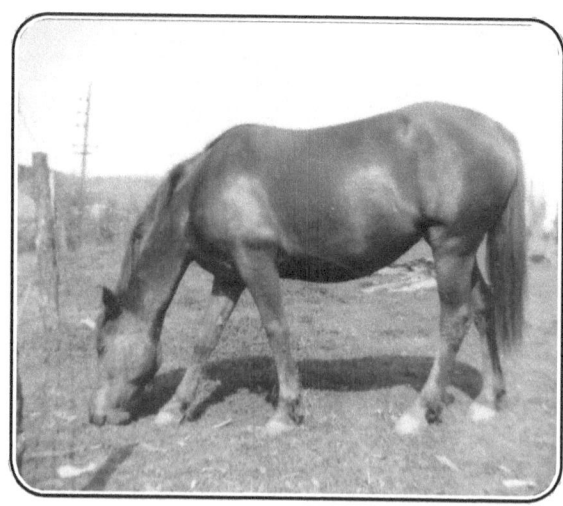

The workhorse, Nellie

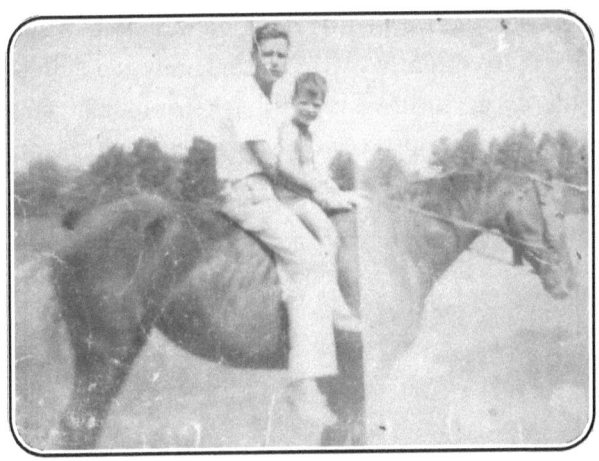

Donald and I riding Nellie

The long days in a cotton field afforded everyone the opportunity to communicate with each other on a full range of subjects. It also allowed us to have a good suntan, sore knees and hands, tired backs, and the need for a good night's sleep at the end of the day. Dad was an old-time farmer type and was at no time going to allow any grass in the cotton field. His determination was so strong that he walked the fields on Sunday afternoon to decide which area we would start on Monday.

The planting was quite different from the processes used today, as in the early years was done with a one-horse planter and fertilizer distributor. The neighborly thing to do then was for the joining farmers to gather at the field of a farmer and all help with the planting. It was only a short time before the cotton plants were up, along with the hot sun, the best ingredient needed for rapid growth of the cotton crop. As a rule, we kids wore only short pants and a straw hat when chopping time came. We did have a few things to look out for, one being the copperhead snake, which were common in our area.

The days were long as we were in the field as soon as the morning chores were done, such as feeding the animals, and we worked until sundown or the field we were working on was clean of all growing plants other than cotton. We were a farm family and didn't question the amount of time involved in keeping everything moving, just as the farmers of today spend endless days repairing, planting, and harvesting the crops.

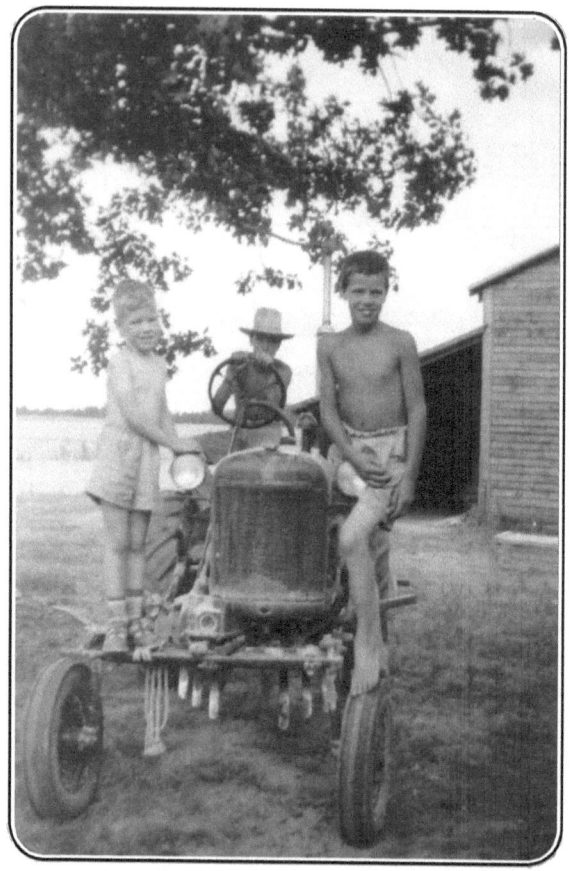

My brother Dick, nephew Steve, and me

After a few years, Dad was able to buy a tractor (Farmall Cub), so now the work could go on after dark as the tractor had headlights on it. The tractor came with a turn plow and cultivators, but most of the other tools had to be converted from horse-drawn to fit the lifts on the tractor. Dad was good at making everything work and had all the horse equipment converted for use on the tractor in short order.

Many things come to mind as I recall those days in the cotton field, like the unmistakable smell of the quart canning jar full of drinking water we kept under the corner of the cotton sheet. Although it was not cool under the cotton sheet, being shaded from the hot sun allowed the water to be slightly cooler than the air. The smell, I am sure, was created in part by whatever had been canned in the quart jar, the sealing rubber around the zinc lid, and the time spent there under the sheet. There is no way to describe that smell, but what I would give to raise that jar to take a drink and recapture that again. This might make you think I am crazy.

I remember those mornings when the dew was heavy and we had to wait until it dried up a little so we could pick. For one thing, the extra weight cost the farmer more to harvest because the pickers were paid by the pound. Also, the moisture would cause the cotton to mildew while waiting for enough to be picked to take to the gin.

One of the unpleasant memories was the worms. Yes, worms. They were called pack saddles, and they were covered with stingers so that, no matter where you touched them, you got quite a sting, which was somewhat painful and needed some attention. It was a good thing if someone in the field was chewing tobacco, as tobacco juice was one of the things that would reduce the pain and slow the swelling.

We also watched out for the stinging worm, which had stingers in the front and back. The front stinger looked like a horn. Both these worms were green and sometimes hard to detect on the green cotton leaves. The tobacco remedy was good for this sting as well. Most of the time when we chopped the cotton, it was very hot, causing discomfort to the feet as we were barefoot most of the time. When it got too hot, we would take a hoe, drag it through the dirt, and step on the freshly cultivated soil to cool our feet.

Then there were the cotton boll fights we got into when picking. Of course, Dad didn't like that part of our horseplay and complained that every boll we threw was a loss of the harvest. As I pass by the cotton fields in Alabama and Tennessee today and see all of the waste due to the method of picking, I can't help but remember how we made sure we gathered every boll with no tags left in the field. A tag was a small amount of cotton that didn't come out of the burr easily and stayed behind. The idea was to look across the field that had been picked and see no white. A job well done was and still is a characteristic of any job done by hand. Of course, nobody picks cotton by hand anymore.

In North Carolina, our method of harvest was somewhat different than cotton growers in other areas. We used what we called tow sacks, or gunny sacks with a strap over our shoulder. We picked every boll of cotton, placed it in the sack, and pulled it along behind us until it was full. When the sack was full, we took it to an area in the field where we emptied it on what we called a cotton sheet made of four gunny sacks sewed together. Each person had his or her own cotton sheet so you could weigh your entire day's picking in the evening. My mother told the story about me at the age of five when we started picking cotton.

I said, "We don't have to do this, do we?"

My dad replied, "Those who don't pick cotton don't eat."

I said, "We don't eat this stuff, do we?"

We picked and emptied our sacks onto this sheet all day. At the end of the day, we tied the corners together and weighed up the sheet to see the total of our accomplishment for the day.

The average pay for picking cotton was about three dollars per hundred pounds, and the amount of a day's work could range from 100 to 350 pounds, depending on how fast you picked. Sometimes it had to do with how much talking went on in the field. Most of the time, that was controlled by the adults picking alongside you. When the sheets were weighed, they were carried to a room in one of the farm buildings to be protected from the weather. They were emptied, and the cotton was held there until enough was picked to make a bale of ginned cotton that would weigh about five hundred pounds after it was baled.

When enough loose cotton was collected, it would be loaded by hand into a wagon or trailer and then hauled to the gin. The ginning process was an experience in itself. A ten- to twelve-inch telescoping pipe was pulled down into the wagon or trailer, and the loose cotton was vacuumed up through the pipe into the gin. The gin removed the seeds from the cotton. Then it was dried and baled. The cotton was then loaded back on the wagon to be taken back to the farm and held until sale time. As a young boy, it was very exciting time when you were allowed to operate the big vacuum tube at the gin.

So what was done with the seed from the ginned cotton? Cotton seed was used for a lot of things, one being ground into a meal and fed to livestock. Real money during this time was not very prevalent, and sometimes the seeds were traded to the gin operator to pay the ginning fees. Some farmers kept seed for the next year's planting. These are some of the memories I have of a young man on the cotton farm in North Carolina.

A daily wage for helping another farmer was three dollars per day. Of course, no pay was expected for working on your own farm.

FOUR

The Corn Patch

Corn was one of the crops we raised, and again, our equipment was limited to the small tractor and trailer. We gathered the corn by hand one ear a time and hauled it to the building we called the granary. It was kept until we used it as feed for the livestock or taken to the hammer mill.

After gathering the ears, the stalks were cut down, and they would be used as cow feed. This is what was known as fodder. Fodder was sometimes left in the field until it was time to feed it, and it was stacked together in stacks, and it was called a corn shock. Shocks were made by using a shock horse made from two-by-fours, and corn stalks were stacked around it. Fodder was also used by taking it to the hammer mill and grinding it up and mixing it with other feed as bulk. Corn was also used for chicken feed after being run through the hammer mill. This feed was called cracked corn, and it was good for the laying hens as well as fat builders.

Most people ate field corn as the very few sweet corn varieties had not been developed at that time. One variety, hickory cane, had a rather large, full ear, and it was a little sweeter than regular field corn. It was a favorite for many, and some farmers planted it to be used for canning. Canning in quart and half-gallon jars was the normal thing to do because very few homes had freezers in them. It was normal for most people to rent a locker at a public locker house

16

in town, and when it was necessary to freeze food, it was put there until needed.

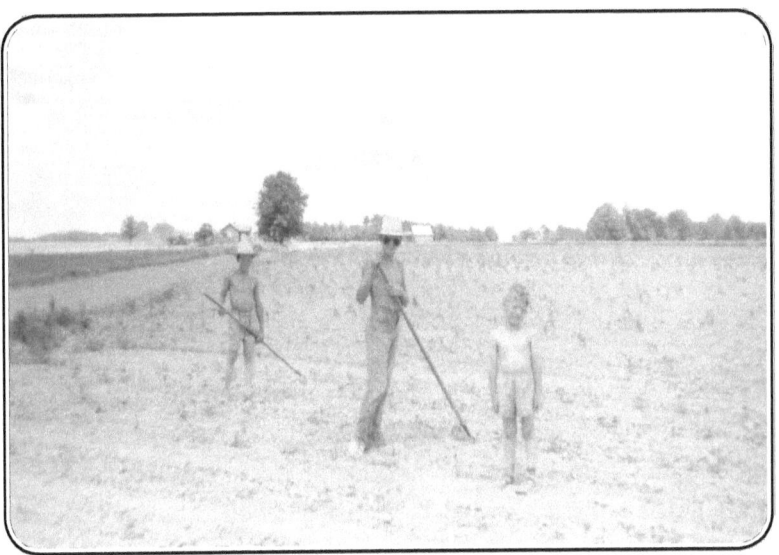

Dick, Steve, and I in the cornfield

FIVE

The Strawberry Patch

Our farm wasn't a very large one compared to most in the area, so to increase the income, Dad decided we should expand our crops to other than the normal row crops other farmers were raising. One of those was a rather large strawberry patch. I don't know if he knew the workload that a big patch of strawberries would put on us or if it would have made any difference had he known. The objective was to sell strawberries and make the farm more productive.

Nevertheless, the patch was set out, and after a lot of cultivating and time, harvest time was here. The berries all had to be picked by hand, and the marketing strategy was to put them in quart baskets, which would be sold on consignment at the store about two and a half miles away. Most people have just a few strawberry plants or a small patch in the garden, but ours was a half-acre or so, and it was the real deal when it came to setting out strawberry plants and picking them for market, with picking being the hardest part.

Copperhead snakes were common in our area, and they seemed to like to hang out in the strawberry patch. I don't know if it was for the birds, insects, or berries, but they were there. The reason I even bring up the strawberries is to explain why I, still to this day, do not like the taste of raw strawberries. I do like preserves, but anybody who knows me would expect that because I like most anything with enough sugar on it.

I was sixteen, and I had only been driving a car a short while when it was up to me to take the berries to the store, driving down a gravel road. Dad had a 1949 DesSto with a fluid drive transmission, which was the family car, and I found out later that it would sell for about three hundred dollars. We loaded the car with berries and placed a quart basket everywhere you could set one—front seat, backseat, and on the floor in front and back, And off I went to the market. About halfway on the crooked gravel road, I lost control, and the car flipped over and over, landing upright in a fence.

When this automobile was built in 1949, seat belts were placed in airplanes, racecars, and the like, but not in family cars. Therefore, when the loaded car flipped, I went bouncing all over the inside, smashing berries everywhere. I fortunately was uninjured in this messy accident, but to look at me, you would have thought I was covered in blood. Naturally, I also caught some berry in my mouth and the taste, which, mixed with the trauma of the situation, has never been forgotten. That is why, even today, I don't like the taste of raw strawberries.

SIX

Strawberries Related to My First Car

— — — — — — — — — — — — —

After rolling over and over, the car landed straddle of the fence. Smashed strawberries covered it all over the inside. After walking about a quarter mile, a lady gave me a ride back to my house. I explained to Dad what had happened, and he said, "Well, we will get the tractor and pull the wreck in." So we did just that. With the top caved in on both sides and every glass broken out, it looked really bad sitting there beside the driveway.

I never will forget what Dad said. "Well, we will go to town in the morning and see what it was worth, and that is what you will owe me."

Morning came, and I can't remember how we got to town. I guess I was still in shock or dulled with anticipation of the debt I owed, but we found out the value of the car was three hundred dollars, and that was my first auto loan. In today's world, the good thing would be that it was a no-interest loan. Now that I had a car, I needed to get it in shape to put on the road. I found out that fixing up the wreck was going to be a task while working for three dollars a day for farmers in the area on my time off.

SEVEN

The Rest of the Story about the Car

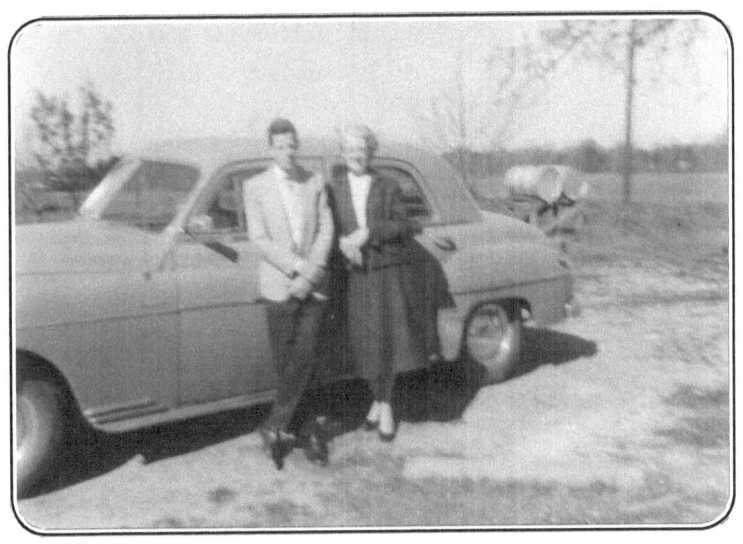

Mother, my 1949 DeSoto, and me

We are talking about a 1949 DeSoto, not such a bad car, but this is, of course, the one with all the windows broken out, the top smashed in on both sides, and strawberries smashed all over the inside, floor, seats, headliner, and all.

Well now, this once nice automobile was mine, although I would be working to pay it off for some time, which meant I wouldn't have any extra money for gas, tires, and so forth. First, I needed to get some new glass for the windows, which I found at the junkyard for a cost of five dollars. Now before the new (used) glass would fit, the opening would have to be put back in shape and alignment.

With the use of a bumper jack extended with a pine four-by-four, the roof was put back in shape so the doors and front window would fit again. I could not go buy the tools needed to straighten the body, so it was done with a hammer and a block of wood. Next was the paint. I did a rather nice job considering I used regular oil-based paint and a cheap paintbrush. I am sure there was a lot of talk about the job not being so professional, but it only had to pass the inspection of one person—me. I knew it had to be done before I could put it on the road, and I am sure that cut down on the time I spent on the job. After all, the overall look wouldn't make it run any better.

Now the old (new for me) car was ready to hit the road. With very limited available dollars, I only went to the necessary places. Now sometimes we would pool our money, and my friends would help with the gas bill. Just a note, gasoline was about twenty cents a gallon. As we all know, tires don't last long, and time came for the need of tires due to a blowout. You guessed it. I had no money for tires. By the way, the tires were nearly gone when the strawberry event happened.

There is an old saying, "A country boy will survive," and in this case, it was so true. Off to the junkyard I went again to keep the wheels turning. Now this was the solution I came up with, and it worked like a charm. Maybe it wasn't that good, but it beat walking.

I got tires one size smaller than the ones on the car and cut the bead off them all the way around so they could be slipped inside the bad tires on the car. Back then, we didn't have tubeless tires, so we turned the bad side of the junkyard tires opposite to the bad side of the ones on the car and put the tubes back in, and off we went.

It was kind of rough and out of balance, but what the heck, I was back on the road.

If you ever saw a nylon tire, you would know that it had several layers of nylon cord and rubber, and when the tire would wear out to the point of a blowout, you could see most of the layers. It looked kind of like a knot in an oak board with the grain showing. It was rather funny when I would stop the car. You could see the worn place in the tire, and someone would say, "You are about to have a blowout."

And as I drove away, I would say, "No, it's okay. Still a few miles left." Little did they know, a whole tire was inside, meaning no chance for another blowout on those tires.

EIGHT

After School at the Sale Barn

— — — — — — — — — — — —

We lived about two and a half miles from a little village called Mineral Springs. This is where I went to school for the full twelve years of my formal education. Mineral Springs is also where we took our wheat and corn to the hammer mill. The town only had one stoplight, and I'm not sure if it was only a caution light in those days. It was also where we took some produce to be sold on consignment.

One of the main events in Mineral Springs was the cattle sale that took place in the big sale barn next to the railroad track. This sale barn was only about a quarter mile from the schoolhouse, and it was a good place after school to pick up a dollar or two for punching livestock through the pens and into the bullpen to be sold by the auctioneer.

I have put a few years behind me now, and I have finally figured out why they used us schoolboys to punch the stock. The process involved using a stick and getting behind everything from young calves to big bulls, hogs to sows with little pigs, and so forth. All of the animals were straight off the farms and under pressure when going down a hallway to the sale pen. Feeling threatened would cause most of anyone of the animals to turn on you, and getting out of the way quickly was important. The only place to go was up on the fence. Another of those very vivid memories was an old sow snapping at your leg on the way up on the fence. If you ever saw an old sow get mad and try to protect her little ones, then you know what I am talking about. If not, it would be hard for me to explain that activity any further.

The big horned bull was another animal that could get pretty testy and take you off your feet if you didn't stay on your toes. I have often thought about the way young folks were allowed to do things that would bring the government agencies down on the parents today. It seems like parents aren't given credit for knowing anything these days, but I will say that, if we had been tested by all of the agencies that the nanny state designs for people, this country would never have been built. (Just sayin'.)

NINE

Moving the Outhouse

— — — — — — — — — — — — —

I will say that everything that was done on the farm was not really pleasant, but most everything we did was necessary, and this was one of those jobs. Most people who were not raised with country connections would likely ask, "What is an outhouse?" Well, believe me, if you ever had to move one, it would be a lasting memory.

For those who don't understand what an outhouse is, I will give you some insight as to what we knew as "the outhouse." First of all, it was there because we had no bathroom in the house. It was the place we went when we needed to go to the bathroom for other reasons than taking a bath. It was a small building with a wooden seat, under which there was a hole in the ground.

As you might expect, over a period of time, the hole would fill up, and the outhouse had to be moved. First, a new hole about four foot square and four feet deep had to be dug by hand with a shovel. A chain was placed around the building, which was attached to the tractor and pulled over the new hole. This, of course, left the old, nearly full hole to be covered up and blocked to stop any further activity around it.

The standard equipment for an outhouse was a bag of lime and the Sears catalog (tissue paper). Quite often, the wasps and mud daubers would build their nests in the outhouse. It had no electricity and no running water, and as I recall, it was a good place to smoke a corn silk cigarette. Corn silk wrapped in brown paper, which was part of a grocery bag, was about as close to a tobacco cigarette as we could get because we did not raise tobacco on the farm, and you could find some corn silk in the corncrib most any time of the year. The next best thing was what was called rabbit tobacco because, I guess, it crumbled up like tobacco in your hand.

It seems like the outhouse was the best place to slip and smoke. You sure couldn't go to the other buildings because you might catch them on fire. I also don't think the smell of smoke would be the dominant smell in the outhouse for long.

There have been a few songs written about the outhouse such as "The Little Brown Shack Out Back" and "The Interstate Is Going Through Our Outhouse." This building also has been the theme of several jokes.

Now this story might not interest you as much as some of the others do, but believe me, it was part of growing up on the farm. And they call these the good old days!

TEN

Working with the Wheat

— — — — — — — — — — — — — —

A book of stories about my younger years on the farm would not be complete without writing about the time I spent working on the wheat thrasher. This piece of equipment was one of things my dad could not afford, so when wheat thrashing time came, we had to bring in a farmer who had the equipment to take care of the crop. As a young man who needed to make some money, about three dollars per day, I was glad to ride the back of the thrashing machine, which a tractor pulled. Riding the back of a thrashing machine doesn't sound like much of a job, but here is the full picture.

The mower would cut about a ten-foot strip of wheat, and the machine would separate the stalk from the head. The stalk dropped off the back. The head (wheat) would go through a cleaning process to blow most of the chaff or husk from the seed. Now, we are talking summertime in the flat country of North Carolina. "Hot" is a word that might come to mind, especially with no roof or umbrella. While moving sacks that weighed a hundred pounds or so, tying the tops so they wouldn't come open when they dropped to the ground causes another word to come to mind, "perspiration." We knew it as sweat.

The chaff or husk from the wheat is separated and flying all around in the air, along with the dust that had settled on the stalk. Of course, we never wore a shirt in the summertime on the farm, which means all those things flying in the air were sticking to my chest and back because of the perspiration. One of the things that made this job more difficult was that you had to leave the filled sacks of grain sitting by the slide and let them go to the ground at the same place every time when you came around the field. This would make it easy to be picked up by the person on the wagon or truck. Wow, what fun.

I compare this to the air-conditioned equipment today and say, "We have come a long way, baby!"

ELEVEN

Farm Activities

All the activities we enjoyed on the farm had to have one thing in common, that is, it must not cost much money and ideally should only cost time, effort, imagination, and ingenuity.

I have thought many times about the one recreation we loved, swimming. There was a pool in town, but it was about six or seven miles away, which was too far to ride a bike because of time limits, even if we had the money to pay to get in, which we certainly did not have. As I think back, I don't think I was ever in the city pool.

Our swimming time was spent going to farm pools in the area. It was always nice to find a pond where the livestock were not using, as it would be much cleaner and the water was clearer. Another favorite pond was one with a willow tree on the bank leaning out over the water so we could climb out and jump in the deeper water.

Some of the area ponds were spring fed, but most were filled with surface runoff water from rainfall. We had a small pond on our farm, which was about ten feet deep at the deepest point in the center. That is where I learned to swim by accident. We were in the water and moving along the edge of the dam. I could not swim, so I was holding on to the grass clumps sticking out of and growing along the dam when suddenly the grass came up by the roots and out into the deep water I went. At that point, it was swim or go down, so I dog-paddled out. From then on, I was able to swim a little and expand my skills without fear of drowning.

We had many a good time in that old pond, and Mom used it to get a lot of work out of us boys by promising to allow us to go swimming when the job was done. We swam in the pond as often as we could until we had a rude awakening one day. The purpose of the water was to water the livestock that ran loose in the pasture and for the pigpen about thirty yards from the pond. The method used to water the pig's watering hole was to carry five-gallon buckets from the pond to the pigpen by hand. That put a whole new light on our most beloved activity. My brother Richard, who was two years older than I was, had gone to the water's edge and dipped up a bucket of water. Much to his surprise, he dipped up a huge water moccasin. This snake was about three feet long and as big around as a pint fruit jar. He came running up to the barn, jumped the bars at the end of the hall of the barn, and came running to the house so excited that he could hardly talk.

"Get the gun! Get the gun!" he said.

We did. That was the end of our swimming in our pond and the beginning of one of the greatest hunting sprees of my childhood. I have forgotten the number of snakes we killed out of that pond, but it was somewhere near the fifty mark. Needless to say, our swimming in the pond came to a screeching halt, but we still went to the other area ponds and did occasionally see a water snake but didn't really worry about them for some reason.

Of course, being boys, we had to have a little fun any time we could, and the snakes did afford us the opportunity once again. My brother-in-law Hoyt was coming to the house, and we decided to get him to walk down to the pond with us to have a look around, having to do with the snake problem, which he was eager to do. We knew in advance that he was coming, so we got the biggest water snake we could find that we had killed and laid it out on the bank of the pond in the path. We walked along the path talking until we approached the snake. To make it look alive, we had taken a small stick and stuck it under its head, which raised it up about two or three inches off the ground.

We had a big laugh when he almost stepped on it, and we yelled, "Look out! There is a big one!"

As think back on this event, I also recall my mother doing the same thing to us with a copperhead near the walk up to the back porch. That may have been payback. I'm not sure.

TWELVE
Seine Fishing Was Legal

There was no law against seining when I was a boy. A seine was made up of a long , large net with a pole on either end. It was pulled through the water by two or more people and the result was a goodly amount of fish being harvested without the use of a fishing line and hook. so that was another pastime we had that also was a source of food. We would seine ponds, creeks, and even the river. The one thing I remember about the river was that the seine would get hung on rocks on the bottom, and someone would have to dive down and clear it from the rock. The seine we used was a net about ten or fifteen feet long and four to six feet high with a pole on either end. Lead weights were on the bottom edge of the net, and cork floats were on the top. The job of keeping the seine free from hang-ups meant you had to follow it, and sometimes, a snake would get stirred up. So guess what was right in its way, the guy behind the seine. I got that job a lot because it was more about swimming than fishing anyway. Of course, the water was all stirred up, and you could not see what was in it until it surfaced.

The story they always told about the old guy who went seining a lot says he always had a bottle in his back pocket. I'm not sure about what was in the bottle, whether it was his own brew or a commercial product, but when asked about it, he said, "Well, you never know when a man might get snakebite, so it pays to have some medicine handy." If someone saw him tip the bottle, he might ask him if he had gotten snakebite, and he said, "No, but I want to keep a little medicine in me just in case."

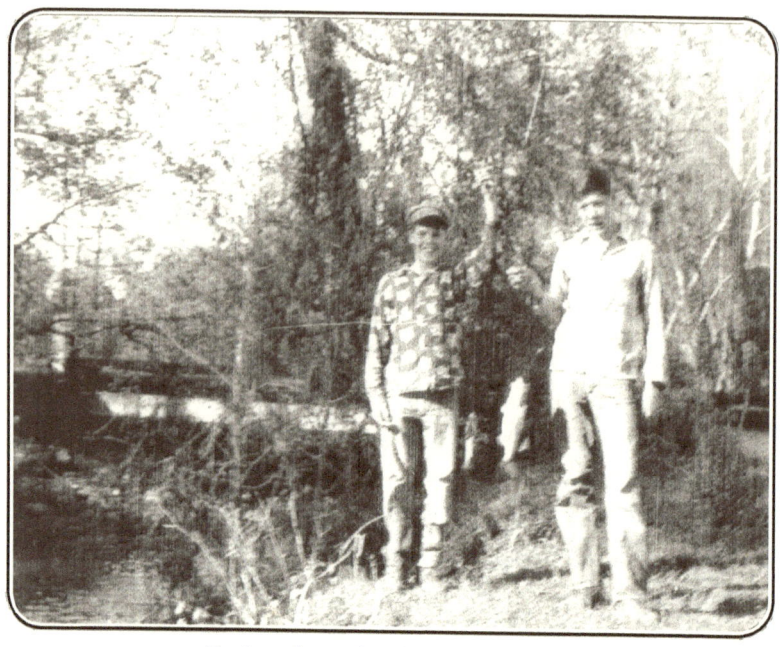

Dick and me after fishing in the creek

THIRTEEN

Fun Fishing the Creeks and Lake

— — — — — — — — — — — —

When our older brother Don was around, we got to go fishing because he liked to fish and knew where to go. Besides, he had a car, and our best transportation was bikes. One place he would take us was a place we called Mecklenburg Creek on the border of the next county about fifteen miles away. This creek was good fishing, and on one occasion, we caught a nice bass and some other fish, so we decided to bring them back and put them in the pond on the farm. With no bucket of any kind, Don came up with a container of some kind, a milk carton or something. We held the fish head down in the container and headed home. We had to stop and get more water out of a mud hole or two to keep it alive. Years later when we seined the pond, there was that big bass.

Another place we liked to fish and did quite often was the lake just outside Monroe, Monroe Lake. It was a great place to fish, but only one motor was allowed in the lake, and the caretaker owned it. The caretaker, Chester Trawick, was the uncle of a famous country singer. Chester was a very nice fellow and would pull us boys up to the upper end of the lake, and we would fish all the way back.

My two brothers, Don and Dick, and I would fish at night, and we used one of the rental wooden, flat-bottomed fishing boats. We would lay crossways off the boat with our heads all on the same side and fish out the other side. There couldn't have been more than three inches between our heads and the water. After thinking about some things we have done, there are a few we would never do again, and knowing now how easy it would have been for a water snake to have gotten in the boat, this is one of those things. I am sure a cold, wet water snake going down one of our collars would have caused some commotion.

We did catch some nice catfish those nights.

FOURTEEN
Frog Gigging, a Summer Pastime

Frog legs can't be found as many places today, and if you do find them, they are from frog farms, and like everything else raised for food, they have a taste that is not the same as the ones we used to gig from the ponds and creeks.

Most all the low areas of the country, creeks, and ponds all had big bullfrogs. Armed with a flashlight and an eight- to ten-foot pole with a gig in the end, we would wade into most any area for a good nest of frogs. Sometimes there would be three or four of us, and together we could gig as much as a quarter of a tow sack full. There's nothing like a fresh mess of fried frog legs from the wild.

Sometimes when we were out in the country at night, we could hear some big frogs, stop, get out the gig, and go wading. I don't know how we managed to go all the places we did and never got snakebite. I guess it proved they were more afraid of us than we were of them. We had a fairly good number of copperhead and cottonmouth snakes in our area also. Sometimes we would us a 22-caliber rifle and hollow point bullets, which worked very well. One night, we were gigging, and I fell in the pond and lost my light and gig as I slipped off the bank. I had to have help getting out, so my buddy reached for me, laughing because I was all wet and muddy. So I gave him a big yank, and in he came, too. It didn't really matter because it was a warm summer night, and staying clean wasn't in our plan anyway.

We seldom went on other people's property without permission, but in those days, most folks didn't care if you gigged their ponds. Funny thing was the respect for other's property seemed to be a lot better than it is today, which resulted in a lot less vandalism.

FIFTEEN
Fresh Milk Daily

_ _ _ _ _ _ _ _ _ _ _

We always had one or two milk cows, mainly for our own use. We made our own butter and all the milk we needed for the family. Sometimes we would have milk to sell. We would put the milk in stainless canisters that a milk truck picked up and took to the local milk distributing company. In addition to milk, butter, buttermilk, and real cream, Mom would make homemade cottage cheese.

All the milking was done by hand, and of course, Mother was very particular with the process to be sure nothing foreign got in the milk, such as flakes from the cow or straw from when the cow when she would switch her tail. Most people would milk with both hands into a bucket, but not Mom. She milked with her right hand into a saucepan, which she held with the left hand and poured into the bucket.

When I was about five or six years old, before I started milking, I would like to squat down beside Mom and watch her while she milked the cow. We always had some cats around the barn to keep down the mice population, and they found out that Mom would give them a squirt or two of milk if they stood around long enough. One Sunday morning she was milking, I was watching when I asked why the cow didn't stand on her whole foot and touch the dewclaw on the left hind foot. Now this was a gentle cow, but she was not used to anything touching her foot, so naturally she kicked. The foot came up hitting the saucepan that was full of milk, sending it straight for me, and like a hat, it landed on my head, which left me covered with warm, fresh milk.

Now warm, fresh milk has a distinct smell, which meant I needed a full bath before going to church, which we did every Sunday morning. Taking a full bath today of course is no big deal, but it was a little different back on the farm. We heated our bathwater in a large teakettle on the stove and took a bath in a number ten washtub. In order to get to church on time, I ended up getting what we called a birdbath, which didn't completely erase the complete smell of milk. Funny how smells stick in your mind forever and some are not so pleasant. By the way, I did become a two-handed milker at an early age.

The bath thing reminds me of our solar-heated shower my brother and I rigged up. I'll tell you about that later.

SIXTEEN

Time to Bring the Outhouse Inside

— — — — — — — — — — — —

When I was about ten years old, Dad decided to put the bathroom in the house, so he got all the necessary equipment needed to do so—a sink, commode, and footed tub. But the one thing we didn't have was a water heater. Our source of energy for cooking and refrigeration was propane gas in one hundred-pound bottles because the house was not wired for 220 volts and a gas water heater was the best way to go.

When we moved to North Carolina, an older brother Ed was left in West Virginia. He had replaced his gas water heater and was able to ship his old one to us, a great improvement over the old teakettle that Mom still used for washing dishes. Now why would she do that if we had installed a gas water heater? We used bottled propane gas, which was too costly to keep the heater going much, so on Saturday evening, Dad would light the heater and heat one tank, about thirty gallons, full of water for everybody's Saturday night bath. We got a full bath every Saturday night, whether we needed it or not. Between Saturday baths is when the "birdbaths" came into play.

Now we were out in the country, so of course, there were no sewer lines to hook to, so we had to first put in a septic tank. Regulation for such a thing was nonexistent, which meant we didn't need to have permits as we do today for perks and so forth. In case you don't know, the perk test is a test on the soil to see if the ground will soak up the water fast enough to make a septic tank work property. Anyway, when we were ready to do the job, we just got on with it.

When we started digging with a pick and shovel, we encountered a rather big problem about eighteen inches below the ground, solid rock. This was really tough to deal with when the only equipment you had was a pick and shovel. As luck would have it, my brother-in-law Simon was somewhat experienced in the use of dynamite. Now dynamite was something you didn't need to mess with if you didn't know what you were doing.

Unlike today, dynamite could be purchased from the local hardware store, and most anybody could get it. A stick of dynamite was about eight inches long, and to adjust the size charge you needed, you cut it with a pocketknife. The fuse came in a roll and was cut to size the same way. It was quite interesting to see the process of selecting the charge and fuse length and then attaching the cap to the fuse, placing the charge in the right place, lighting the fuse, and watching the huge rocks go flying into the air. The hard part still to come was getting all the rocks out of the hole. This, of course, was done by hand. The field line had to be dug also by hand, but believe me, we were proud to have a bathroom in the house, and the effort was well worth it.

I heard a story about an old couple who had never had a bathroom in the house so the old man told his wife he was going to close in the porch and make a bathroom there.

She said, "Oh no, you are not bringing that mess in this house."

A saying my mother used to use was, "Poor folks do poor ways." Looking back, that applied to a lot of things we did.

SEVENTEEN

Our Use of Solar

We were always coming up with some kind of idea to make things better without spending much money. We did get a tub in the house for our Saturday night bath, but while working in the fields and barn area, we sometimes got rather dirty so we needed to get cleaned up. We figured that a shower outside would be mighty nice, a lot better than a birdbath, so we went to work on a plan. We located an old tub that we could put a valve in and placed it on top of the roof over the bathroom, which was a porch prior to closing it in, and it was only about nine feet or so off the ground. We attached a short piece of old hose pipe to the valve and a bottle sprinkler on the other end, which hung down to about six feet off the ground.

With buckets, we filled the tub on the roof in the morning and let the sun heat the water all day so we would have a warm shower in the evening. Now it took some work to do all this, but it worked pretty well. We didn't call it a solar water heater, but with the heat from the sun, that is exactly what it was.

EIGHTEEN

The Toys of Our Day

It may seem strange to some and certainly hokey to the younger folks who were born after the 1950s, but we made most of our own toys, which caused us to be more creative and increase our skills and abilities to make something from nothing. Of course, you might ask, "What kind of toys did we have?" Let me try to make you understand my claim of creation.

Crystal Radio

Of course, we had no such thing as a personal radio, transistor radios, personal record players, stereos, iPods, or personal tape recorders. This was before reel-to-reel tape recorders, eight-track tapes, cassette recorders, and digital recorders, and only the select few had access to TV sets. I did see a reel-to-reel recorder that used a fine wire, but I believe that was only used by commercial recording companies and was not for normal home use. For the most part, only the well-to-do, as my mom would say, could afford to have any of these things as they came on the market. As you might have surmised, we were not among the well-to-do.

In about 1951 or 1952, due to the knowledge of my older brothers (which was passed on to me), I learned to make a crystal set radio. If you haven't seen a crystal radio or understand about radio waves, it might be hard to believe that a radio can be made from a double-edged razor blade or a piece of quartz crystal, safety pin, some fine copper wire, a toilet paper roll, an antenna, a grounding system, and an earphone. Believe me, it can because I went to sleep every night listening to WBT Radio in Charlotte, North Carolina. This radio took no batteries or electrical current whatsoever, only an antenna (the screen on the bedroom window or the springs on the bed) and a ground wire (attached to a pipe that had been driven into the ground outside the window). It was able to pick up the station with the most power or the closest to the radio. The memories are very clear of Edward R. Murrow, Walter Cronkite, Author Smith, and the Cracker Jacks, to name a few along, with all the latest musical hits.

We were not among the wealthy, so the material needed to make a radio was not easy to come by. For Christmas, my older brother Don got a set of earphones and gave it to my other brother and me, one of the best gifts I ever received, which we separated by giving us one earphone each to use on our own radio. Now the earphones were made out of Bakelite and got very cold in the wintertime. In order to fix the problem, we thinned out our feather pillow in the center and placed the earphone under the pillow, allowing us to listen to the radio on those cold winter nights as we had no heat in the bedrooms. In fact, sometimes we had window ice up to a half-inch thick. We figured that the length of the antenna had something to do with the reception we could get on the radio, so I decided to hook it to the telephone line. Sure enough, it worked fine, but I found out really quick that Dad would not allow that, so my long antenna idea was short-lived.

It is easy nowadays to buy toys made of almost every kind of material known to man, many of which have been developed years later than my days as a boy. Our small cars and trucks we had were made from wood and cut down to resemble whatever we thought would be an interesting design. The wheels were made from an old broom handle, or if it was for a tractor, we would make from a tree limb with the bark still on so it would make tracks in the dirt. If we could find paint, we would paint the toys, and if not, pokeberries and the like made good dye.

We also made what we called tractors by cutting notches in the rim of a wooden spool, placing a rubber band through the hole held on one end by a piece of matchstick and on the other in a stick about one and a half inches long with a piece of wax crayon between the stick and the spool. Twisting the stick would tighten the rubber band, and when placed on the ground, it would cause the spool to travel under its own power. We would see who could make the most powerful tractor and have a contest.

Another rubber band-powered toy was a paddleboat we built in several variations and sizes. A rubber band could be made by cutting a section of an old bicycle tube or an automobile tube, which worked very well. We also used the inner tubes for slingshot rubber. A block of wood like a two-by-four with a thin strip of wood fastened to each side extending far enough past the end to accommodate a four-piece paddle was a fun way to make the paddleboat. The idea was to make it look like the old riverboats, and believe it or not, they worked and added hours of pleasure to our pastime.

Making Homemade Checkers

An old broom handle served as the material for making checkers cut off in about a quarter-inch slices. They could be stained with walnut bark and pokeberries.

Our Flying Jenny

One of our favorite big toys was what we called the flying jenny, which we made by cutting down a tree about thirty inches or so above the ground with a crosscut saw on about a twenty- to thirty-degree angle, after which a hole was drilled in the center with a handheld wood auger big enough to put a cross arm bolt that is about three quarters inch by fifteen inches. On top of the tree stump was placed a wooden board (two by ten by twelve or fourteen) with a hole in the center where the cross arm bolt was placed going down into the stump about eight or ten inches. Axle grease was placed between the tree stump and the wooden board to make it spin freely on top of the tree stump.

One person would get on each end of the board and start spinning round. The slant that cut on the tree stump would cause the wooden board to go up and down as you went around. By the way, no motor or motion was created by pushing yourself around by your feet when you were on the lower side of the spinning board. We enjoyed lots of Sunday afternoons on the flying jenny.

Riding Down the Hickory Trees

Another activity we had was not really a toy. We just took advantage of the tools that Mother Nature provided us. We would find a hickory tree from fifteen to thirty feet tall, climb up to the top, hold on, swing out, and ride it to the ground. It was kind of like bungee jumping, I think.

Sometimes we would find a bigger tree, and the two of us would climb to the top together and, at the same time, swing out to ride it down. I will never forget one time we were riding the big tree down, and Dick, my older brother, turned loose and dropped to the ground before I did, and I went sailing back up in the air. I held on to the tree, which left me hanging up there, too far up to drop and too low to get back up the tree. I never did know if he did that on purpose or if it was an accident. Either way, there was only one thing to do, climb back up the tree and help me weigh it down enough to get off safely. So that was what he did. Everything turned out okay, but the next time we did a big tree, we counted, one, two, three, drop.

Tom Walker Stilts

Stilts, sometimes called tom walkers, were also homemade, and we became rather adventurous in this area. We started with short heights of about a foot and finally went to the extreme of about eight feet so we could sit in the barn loft and mount our stilts. The real skill came when we were dismounting. I will not describe some of the not so graceful dismounts, so you can picture that in your own mind.

I'm thinking what a shame there was no video of some of the stuff we did. It would have made funniest videos and some mighty good shows, but on second thought, it's probably good it's not on film for the kids to try stuff like it is.

Our Covered Wagon

How many kids have you known that have taken a one-horse wagon, made arches from hickory poles, and covered them with cotton sheets? We attached ropes to the shafts to be guided from the front seat and then turned the wagon loose down the hill with no horse. Now riding down the hill was fun, but the interesting part was when we couldn't get stopped before hitting the creek bank. All I can say is that we were among the luckiest kids alive.

The wagon did turn over, breaking the hickory arches, and the bed came apart from the wheels, but it is one of the more memorable experiences of a country boy's life. This was one of many things I would advise kids not to try.

NINETEEN

Billy the Favorite Goat

— — — — — — — — — — — —

Billy wasn't a toy. Rather, he was a pet goat, but I have to include him in my stories about my youthful years on the farm.

We always had cows, pigs, chickens, ducks, a horse, cats at the barn, dogs, and so forth. But it was a happy day when Billy the goat came to add some fun to life around the farm. Billy was a young male goat, and he was quite a pet. Dad had a leather harness made for Billy so we could hook him to a small wagon. We taught Billy to play hide-and-seek. One of us would hold our hand over his eyes while everybody found a hiding place in the rain barrel, in the corncrib, or behind a tree or someplace like that. After counting to fifty, we would turn Billy loose, and he would look in all the spots around the house and barn. When he found someone, he would stand on his hind legs and say "Baa Baa." Then he would find someone else. As he got older, Billy grew horns and learned to stand on his hind legs and go headfirst into whatever was in his way. When we had new people around, he found his mark if someone bent over to go under the fence. Luckily, no one was injured with this little game, although we did bet some torn jeans.

Billy was quite an active goat and loved to get out of the fence or off the rope he was tied to anytime he could. One of the mischievous things he would do, which was the most aggravating to my mother, was to head straight for any flower that was blooming and eat it. He seemed to like the taste, but we decided that he knew he was not to have them. We decided it was all to aggravate our mother because he didn't eat the blooms from anything inside his fence.

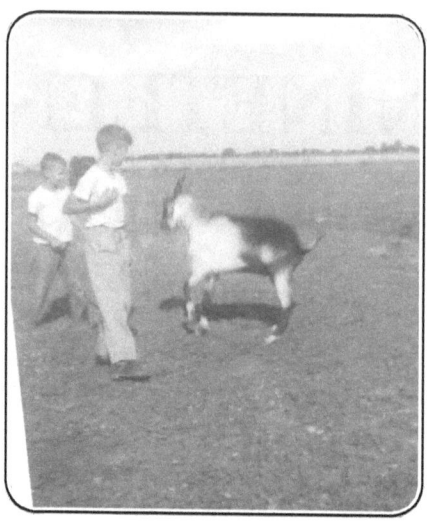

Dick and me playing with Billy

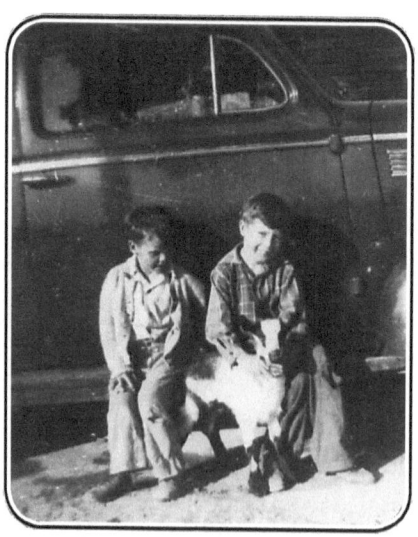

Dick and me with Billy as three kids

TWENTY
The Country Walkie-Talkie

From the loft of the barn to the loft of the granary was about a hundred feet. These two places made a great hideout for a young boy, and ideally, there should be a method of communications between the two places. Today, two boys might likely have a set of warlike talkies or even a cell phone.

Naturally, that technology or means was not available, so we went with the best method available to us, a walkie-talkie made with two bean cans, a cotton string, and a bit of rosin from a sweet gum tree. It sounds primitive, and it was, just as many other things we did, but it worked.

First, we took the paper off two bean cans and punched a hole in the end of each one. We would find two plastic buttons and a string long enough to go from one building to another. Running the string through the hole in the end of the can and attaching it to the button would hold the string in place. This was done on each end, and the string pulled tight. In order to allow the string to carry the sound from one can to another, we would get a gob of rosin from a sweet gum tree and apply it to the full length of the string. By talking into the can on one end and someone placing an ear on the other can, you could communicate very well.

I was always happy when I got to drive the tractor up the road to the country store at Houston where, as I remember, gas was nineteen cents per gallon and a soft drink was five cents. Funny that I would remember that, but I do recall when the price of a drink went up to six cents. One of the farmers was complaining about the penny and said it would never fly. He said that people wouldn't pay that much for a Coke. Cheerwine was one of my favorite drinks back then. I am sure that not getting very many of them had something to do with it.

I don't know how old I was when we got a phone put in, but I remember the event clearly. They had to build a line with poles, all before we could get a phone, and with that, it was a seven-party line. The same phone line went to seven houses, and everybody was on that line and could listen in to all the conversations from all seven houses. Sometimes you might have to butt in and ask a neighbor to let you have the line to make a call. Everybody had his or her own ring, like a long and a short, three longs, and so forth.

When the man came to install our phone, I was sitting out in the front yard, and my mother was cutting my hair, as she had done all my life and did until I was in high school. The man said he could cut hair, and Mom gave him the scissors. He finished cutting my hair on company time. Later on when I got a job with the electrical company, I rode to work with that same man, and he still worked for the phone company.

TWENTY-ONE

The Hay Field

We operated a farm, as were most of the farmers in the area, so our way of doing things was mostly the small farmer way, which resulted in less than enough equipment to do any job the quick and easy way.

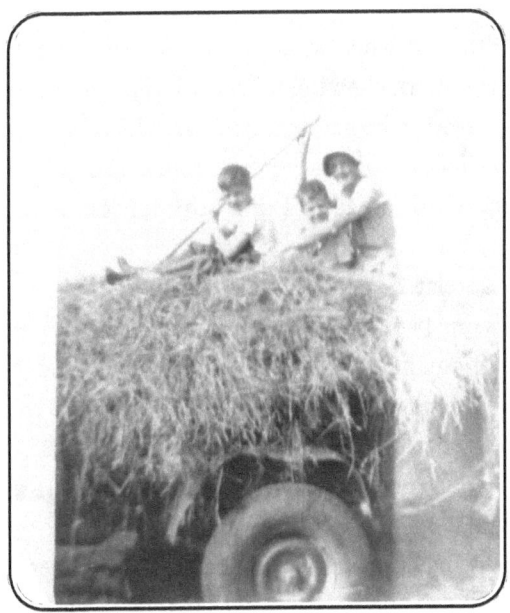

Mother, Dick, and me on the hay trailer

We did have some big farmers around who were equipped with hay balers, wheat thrashers, corn pickers, and so forth. With no baler, we hauled our hay loose using pitchforks and a small trailer pulled with the family car until Dad got the Farmall Cub tractor. Now I grant you there was some talk about the farmer who used the family as a tractor, but I don't think we really cared because it was much easier than a horse and wagon.

Before the tractor, I was quite small and not able to pitch the hay up on the trailer or into the barn loft, so I got to be up on the trailer or in the loft to pack the hay when Mom, Dad, or my brothers would pitch it up. Later on when I was big enough to use a pitchfork, my brother and I would pitch a double load up together, and my dad was in the loft pitching it back and packing it. I remember him saying, "Boys, if you could pitch it a little further back, it sure would help."

It is said that you shouldn't tell it all, and that is probably right, but I'm telling this one anyway. My brother Don, who is ten years older, was in the loft when we were hauling hay one time and had a block of a Days Work chewing tobacco. I asked him for a chew, and much to my surprise, he gave me a pinch, which of course made me rather light-headed, more like green around the gills. This was my first experience with tobacco. I don't think Mom ever knew about that one.

This is not related to hauling hay, but because I am telling it all, I will tell this one because it is too good to keep. We always loved to shoot a gun of any kind and did so quite often. One day, my older brother Don, the same guy with the tobacco, and I were going to do some target practice and made a stack of targets to use. We took the targets and nailed them on a post so when we shot three rounds or so we could take one target off the top and shoot the second target. I don't know why either one of us, being as intelligent as we were, figured the bullet would go all the way through, but when we pulled the first target off, we found out they all had been used. We kind of said we were not going to tell that one, but what the heck. It's a good story.

TWENTY-TWO

Mineral Springs and the Hammer Mill

As you can tell, the life on the farm was somewhat different than the life of young men and ladies living in the city or town. Another of the differences was that we raised most of our food and meats. In doing so, we had the upper hand on fresh foods and foods that had not gone through the processing procedures of the canning companies.

Our flour came from the wheat from the fields, as did the cornmeal from corn raised on the farm. The choice ears of corn were selected. Some was saved for seed for next planting, and some was saved for the cornmeal and grits.

Going to the hammer mill was always exciting for me for some reason. I guess it was because we didn't go much and the process that took place was just something that a boy would enjoy. Mineral Springs was a small place, kind of a wide spot in the road with one caution light where the county school was located, a couple stores, and a café right on the railroad located about two and a half miles away. That was where we would take the corn and wheat to the hammer mill to be ground and put into large cans we called lard stands. They were called lard stands because everybody used them to store lard taken from the fat of the hog after the slaughter. This was another process we went through while laying back food supplies.

TWENTY-THREE

Slaughtering the Hog

This is as good time as any to talk about the hog slaughter. The process started about four in the morning when Dad would start the ball rolling by killing the hog. Water had to be heated in a large, black iron pot in the yard with a wood fire. The hot water was used to scald the hair from the skin. After the hams and shoulders were removed, the rest of the hog was cut up, and the fat, along with the skin, was boiled down to lard, meat skins, and cracklings. Now it was time to use the lard stands to store the lard, which Mom used for cooking. Lard took the place of the things we now use, such as Crisco, corn oil, and so forth.

Now some would argue that the biscuits, cornbread, and pie crust made from the flour, cornmeal, and lard are not good for the health of a person, but I can say for sure that the taste far exceeds most of today's healthy cooking recipes. It's been years since I've had something we called crackling cornbread. Cracklings were the small parts of fat left in the cooker after rendering the lard. Little, crisp pieces of almost burned fat were cooked into the cornbread, and man, was it good.

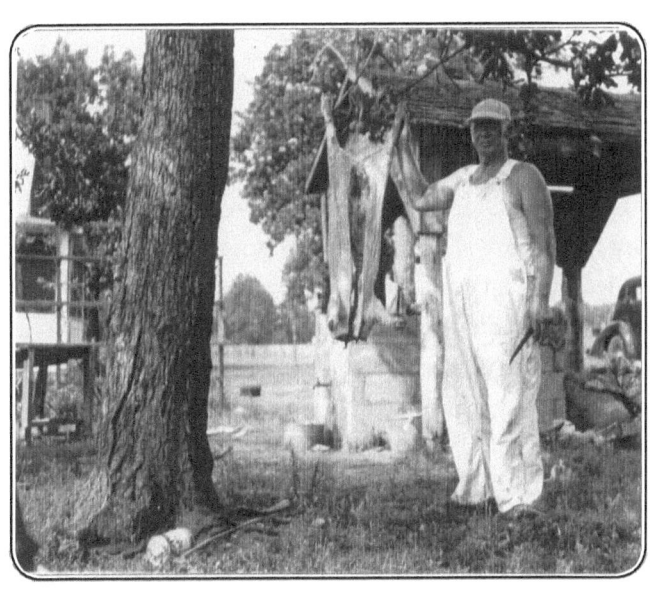

Dad preparing the pig

TWENTY-FOUR

Saving Seed

– – – – – – – – – – – – – – –

When I talked about the hammer mill, I mentioned the way we saved the corn seed for the next crop, but that was not the only seed we saved. I am sure all kinds of seeds were available from the seed companies, but that only added to the cost of planting. All cost had to come from the sale of the product, and, in most cases, profits were small, and all extra cost had to be dealt with. Adding to the workload of a farmer was saving as much seed as possible from your best yield of corn, lespedeza, okra, cucumber, pumpkin, watermelon, tomato, and so forth. Again, most all this was done by hand. We did have an attachment for the mower to catch the lespedeza seed.

Another crop we added to the truck farming idea was okra. The funny thing about okra, most people in the South loved it, and very few in the North even knew what it was. Dad decided to plant about an acre of okra to sell to the local markets. This crop required a lot of attention when it came to keeping the grass out of the rows and even more when harvest time came. If you don't know okra, you need to know it has to be picked no less than every three days, or the pod will get too hard to cook. If left on the stalk too long, it will quit bearing. If you kept it picked, it would bear almost to frost. The bad thing was that when you picked it, you got little stickers on your hand that you could hardly see but that would itch like crazy. My sisters, Dorothy and Wanda, would sing, "I've been working in the okra, all the live long day" to the tune of "I've Been Working on the Railroad." The words were made up as they went. We all had to do something to pass the time, and singing while working in the field was one of them.

The last of the okra was left to go to seed, and we kept it in sacks to be shelled by hand for planting next year. I think part of the reason for shelling all that okra was to keep us busy during the winter. We ended up that year with a huge amount of seed that we could never plant, but we found they were just right to be used in a peashooter. This gave us an endless supply of ammo. We also found that a drinking straw at school made a cool peashooter. I am afraid the teachers didn't think it was too cool.

TWENTY-FIVE

You Can't Hide Seed
in the Ground

— — — — — — — — — — — — — —

I really don't know how old I was, but I was old enough to be planting seed in the garden with my brother. We had saved an overabundance of okra seed, and we were to plant a certain amount. When we finished, we could go to the house. When we got to the end of a row, I figured I would just bury the remaining seed at the end so we could quit. Well, I did just that, and everything was fine until about four or five days later when they all came up at once.

Dad said, "Well, I see where you tried to hide the seed, but it didn't work."

I think he told everybody that came around about that deal.

It is hard to live something like that down.

TWENTY-SIX

Drawing Water from the Well

— — — — — — — — — — — — —

When we moved to the old farmhouse, there was no bathroom, telephone, heat except for a fireplace, or, of course, running water. We had two wells in the back rather close to the house. One was a dug well, which was mostly surface water and about twenty-five or so feet deep and about thirty-two inches across.

The other well was the one we were to use for our cooking, drinking, and bathwater. Now if you have never been exposed to what was known as mineral water, you will never understand this situation. The funny thing is that the people who lived here from childhood loved the water. On the other hand, we had moved from West Virginia where the water was rather good, so the new water was quite a shock to our taste buds.

Water, like many other things, was something we didn't waste. A fresh bucket of water was kept on a shelflike banister on the back porch that was near the well. Near the bucket was a porcelain wash pan where we would wash up before entering the house. A tin dipper was always hanging near the bucket for anyone needing a drink. It seems we all used the same dipper, and that was just the way it was.

The well with the mineral water was a drilled well with a steel casing about six inches across. With the dug well, we could use a regular galvanized water bucket on the end of a rope to get the water from the well. On the other hand, the bucket for the drilled well was what we called a baler, and it was a cylinder about three feet long with a release valve on the bottom of it. It was made of tin. This would be lowered into the well by a rope from a roller and a crank, which we called a windlass. Now according to my dad, it was called a windlass because most of the old wells used a tower with a windmill on top that was used to pump the water, and without the windmill to turn the pump, it was called a windlass. I later learned that the windlass was called that because it came from the word *wind* as "any of various machines for hoisting or hauling." We had to crank up the baler to get the water because we had no electricity or a wind-driven pump.

After a while, we did get an electric pump, but that didn't work well either because the well would go dry if we used too much water. The answer to that was rationing.

One very important thing to remember about the windlass was that if you let go of the crank handle, the baler would fall, picking up speed toward the bottom of the well. Trying to stop the crank could and most likely would result in a serious injury or even a broken bone.

Funny thing about those days, your thought processes controlled the safety measures. With all the safety controls of today that we didn't have then, we must have been mighty lucky or used our thought processes very well. It seems the government must not have figured we were as stupid as the government does today. Just a thought.

This mineral water would build up in the buckets and look like rust. I often wondered if it was good for us or if it did cause things like kidney stones and so forth. We did use the water from the dug well for the washing, which was done in the yard or in what we called the washhouse or on the back porch. This water was known as soft and good for washing. The mineral water was hard, and it would hardly make suds with soap. We also used the water from the dug well for our solar shower. With no water heater, you might wonder how we washed in hot water. We had a big, copper-lined, black pot where we heated water with a wood fire. You would think with these memories of water usage that we would conserve, but I don't think that was the case.

The dug well was also used to refrigerate things like watermelon, milk, butter, cream, and so forth. There is nothing like pulling up a tow sack with a watermelon that has been down in the cold well water for a few days. It's hard to beat a good watermelon that is cold all the way through.

If you know anything about sour mash, you would relate it to making whiskey, but in our case, we fed it to the hogs to help them gain weight. We kept two barrels next to the dug well where we put in ground feed, filled it with water, and let if ferment. While it was fermenting, we fed the hogs out of the other barrel. It's a heavy thing, a five-gallon bucket of hog feed (slop).

TWENTY-SEVEN

Toby

‒ ‒ ‒ ‒ ‒ ‒ ‒ ‒ ‒ ‒ ‒ ‒ ‒ ‒

We always had a dog or dogs of some kind, mostly what we called Sooners. If you have never heard that term in relationship to dogs, it means it could be sooner one breed or another. This meant we had no idea of the background of the dog. I don't think we ever had a dog with papers while on the farm, but we had some great dogs.

The most memorable dog was what we believed to be mostly a bluetick hound mixed with something else, which would make him a sooner. One thing for sure, whatever mix he was, he had a good head and a good mouth, and he was a very smart dog. Toby was our best friend, and he would take up for my brother and me most anytime we needed him to. As I traveled my ten miles on my *Grit* paper route, which I ran every Saturday by bicycle, Toby would be right by my side.

I am sure a lot of people have never heard of the *Grit* paper, but it was a neat little paper that I sold for ten cents a copy. Ten cents a copy didn't add up to much money, but in the fifties, you were lucky to get that. As a salesman, I got four cents per copy and ended up with about one dollar most of the time I ran the route. Think about it, a soft drink was only five cents, snacks were five cents, and so on. If you had a dollar in your pocket, you were doing okay. I also sold garden and flower seed on the bike, so the basket in the front of my bike was well used.

Now, every so often, I would encounter a new dog on the route, and old Toby had to teach it a lesson, to stay on the porch while we passed, and he did his job well. He seemed to have no problem with size, and he would take on anything that was a threat to me on the bike.

The animal rights people would no doubt be on my case if I were armed with a water gun filled with ammonia like I did back then. The ammonia gun was my backup if there were more than two dogs. With one shot in the face, the attacking dogs would get out of our way pretty fast. I kept the water gun in the basket over the front wheel with the extra papers to be delivered.

Now Toby hardly ever went out in the road in front of our house when someone came by, but as soon as they came in the yard, he was on the job. Again, he was good at it. Most people would not test him, and that was a smart move. Funny thing, he would lay there and never move his head, only his eyes, but he saw every move that was made. He was a dog that would bite but only if he had a reason, to protect us.

Sometimes he would take a piece of rope in his mouth with the other end tied to the bike and pull us down the road to the store.

When we moved from the farm, after I had graduated from high school, Toby got really sick. Dad said he had cancer and had to put him out of his misery. It was a hard thing to do, but everyone agreed he was better off.

It is often said that a dog is a man's best friend, and Toby surely was that.

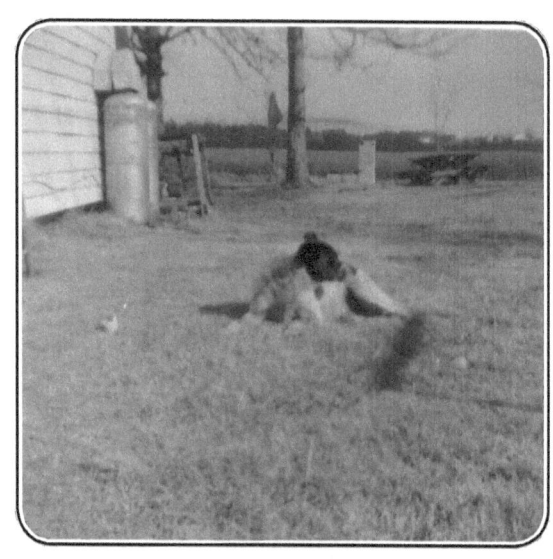

Toby, my best dog

TWENTY-EIGHT

The Smokehouse

Because we raised our own meat on the farm and Dad had his own way of preserving, we needed a smokehouse. I don't know of anyone who has a smokehouse in our area now, but it was necessary for us in order to eat as well as we did. There were many things we did not have, but food was not one of them.

The shoulders, hams, sides, and sausage would be hung from the rafters. An open fire was built in the building, and the smoke cured the meat. I can't recall how long it took to preserve the meat, but I do remember Mom going out to the smokehouse with a butcher knife to cut off a slice of meat for whatever meal she needed it for. Believe me, it made for good eating.

Smoking was not the only way that meat was preserved. There was salt curing, liquid smoke, and sugar curing, all of which resulted in some mighty fine meat with just a different taste. Mom and Dad seemed to know all the ways to preserve food, and I guess they learned it when they were children. Mom grew up in the West Virginia mountains from 1900 to the 1920s and then moved to Huntington, West Virginia. Dad lived in the farm country of North Carolina from 1898 to 1915 or so when he left home and worked as a cook on a ferryboat on the outer banks of North Carolina.

We canned everything. As the old saying goes, we killed a hog and kept everything but the squeal. But nothing ever goes exactly as planned. One time, Mom was canning sweet potatoes, or it could have been tomatoes, and the jars exploded. She was burned badly on her neck and had scars forever. It nearly scared us all to death, but she always said, "Where there is a will, there is a way," and we made the best of it.

With no freezer, everything had to be put up in glass jars, and if it's not done just right, it will spoil and cause serious illness or death. Thank goodness, they knew what they were doing because we had such good eats, if you know what I mean. Besides, if they didn't, we might not be here to tell about it.

We kind of got away from the smokehouse, but I think it all goes together and was a part of life in the forties and fifties.

TWENTY-NINE
The Joys of Camping

My brother Dick, who was two years older than I was, and I would get the urge to spend the night in the woods, so we would each roll up a blanket along with a few other things like a flashlight, some matches, a jar of water, and whatever we could confiscate from Mom's kitchen. And off we went into the wild like two men on safari. It seemed not to bother us that, along the way, we were sure to cross over or at least pass by a snake or two. We also knew that, once in a while, a wild cat (bobcat) could be heard in the area. Of course, we had Toby with us.

We would move the leaves and grass back with a rake and make a place to lie down on our blankets. We would also make a circle of rocks about two feet across where we could build a small fire. We also sometimes stopped by a pond and caught a fish or two to cook over the fire on a stick. Cooked frog legs made a good late night snack. We cooked on a stick as we never took any cooking utensils with us. Taking silverware from Mom's kitchen wasn't even considered. There were no plastic throwaway forks, knives, or spoons at that time that we knew of, so we did without so as not to take the chance of losing anything. Sleeping out under the stars was a great thing to do as a boy, and sometimes we would just stay in the yard if we were not going to meet somebody else who was going with us.

We made our own hammocks out of whatever we could find. We used anything from fence wire to barrel slats woven together with twine. Dick found a jungle hammock at a used army/navy store for five dollars and kept it hanging between two trees in the backyard. In the summer, we slept out there more than in the house. With no air conditioning in the house, it was much cooler outside.

When Dick woke up one morning after sleeping in the hammock, his head was on the ground, and his feet were still up in the air. Someone had come up during the night, cut the rope on the head end, and let him down so easy that he didn't even wake up. He always thought I had something to do with it, but it had to be some of his friends who didn't have a nice jungle hammock for themselves. We always kidded him about being a sound sleeper.

During this time, we didn't have plastic sheets or fancy bags to carry our stuff in or to lay down on the ground under the blankets. If it rained, we got wet. In an effort to upgrade our camping experience, we decided to build a lean-to in the edge of the wooded area of the farm. We went to work cutting some pine poles with the ax and crosscut saw and lashed them together with grapevines. Pine branches full of needles were used to make a roof, and believe it or not, it kept the rain off.

Sometimes we would hike to the homes of some other boys, and they would join us in the camp. Memories of lots of fun-filled nights surround our adventurous attitude.

We were known to make a stop by our girlfriends' houses, another reason to get started early. Of course, that was the part we didn't tell everybody.

I know you would like to know more, but that's the end of that story for now.

THIRTY

School Days

When I started to school in 1948, not much attention was directed to whether a child was in school every day or not. This was mostly left up to the parents. The reasoning behind this was that most of the families in the school system were farmers, and without the equipment available today, most everything was done by hand or at least what we would now call the hard way.

We had been in our new home (old farmhouse) in North Carolina for only a short time when school started. It was my first year. All the other kids were already going to school, and now my mother would be left alone on the farm with very few new friends. So it seemed that keeping me home would be a good thing to do, especially if I might not be feeling well on any given morning. You would think it would be a relief to send all the kids to school and have some time to herself, but you must understand that she had been home with kids in the house daily for twenty-five years. (Mom had a child every two years for twenty years. I was the youngest of ten.)

I don't remember this, but she said many times that she would ask on the mornings she would like me to stay home was, "You don't feel like going to school today, do you?" Of course, the answer was no. This was first grade because there was no kindergarten or early schooling at that time.

Needless to say, if given the chance to stay home, I was ready. Therefore, my attendance record was not too good for my early school years. Some other things were interesting about my school. The elementary and high school were next to each other, and most of us that started in the first grade finished together in grade twelve. The building for the elementary school was an old two-story building with four rooms upstairs and four rooms downstairs with a stairwell on either end. This building had been condemned for safety reasons, but it was fixed by putting six-by-six timbers in several places in the lower rooms of the building.

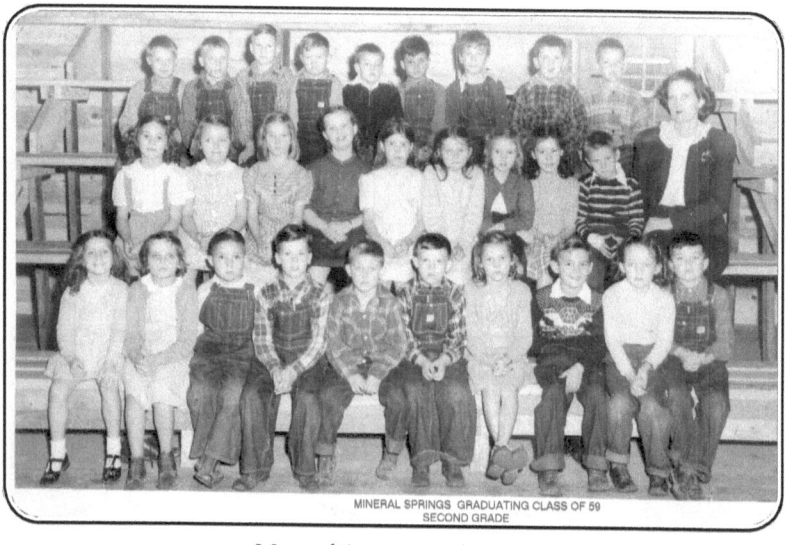

MINERAL SPRINGS GRADUATING CLASS OF 59
SECOND GRADE

Mineral Springs High School

The high school students drove the buses. You must remember that this was 1947 to 1959, and the safety features were none compared to today's standards. I can recall old bus #99. Now this bus smoked like an old lawnmower, and the seats were bench seats that ran front to back on the bus. When you got on the bus, you sat down on the front of the seat. When someone else got on, you slid back, and he or she sat down in front. The seats in the center had no back, so whoever was behind you was back to back. I can hear the bus driver now saying, "Scoot it on back! Scoot it on back!" And you sat down and shut up.

No one was allowed to stand up on the bus or to be loud. There were no hands out the window. Along with every student bus driver, another person was assigned to each bus, and we called that person a "tail twister." The job of the tail twister was to keep an eye on everybody and report to the school office anything that was not to take place on the bus. It was not a good thing to be reported by the tail twister because, back then, you were set up for a whipping pretty quickly. Some of the teachers and principals had very little mercy when rewarding you for misguided actions.

Most classes had about twenty students, and most grades had two classes that would make the graduating classes run in the forties. Only a few students drove to school while all the rest rode the bus. The average family had one car, and some had none, so the school buses were the best way to get there. If you were close enough, you could ride a bike. We did this sometimes as we were about two and a half miles away. There seemed to be no problem with the people who drove to school. If they had a personal firearm, it was left in the car or truck.

Several roads were gravel and very little of that, leaving a lot of mud when it rained. Some were so bad that, if it rained a lot, school would go on a rainy day schedule and get out early so the buses could get the kids home. If they got stuck, they would have plenty of time. On occasion, buses were known to get stuck in the middle of some of the worst roads.

The discipline plan was good enough that most kids found that not obeying the rules wasn't worth it. Smoking was allowed for high school students, but you had to have a note from a parent, and it was only allowed in one area at the end of the high school building under a tree called the smoking tree.

We played several games at school, including baseball, football, basketball, marbles, can lid war, foot racing, girl watching, horseshoes, and so forth. The sports were like most schools. There was a clique in each area for which we had our own names. But when it came to marbles and horseshoes, we took it seriously. This one kid had cut a hole in the heel of his shoe, and when he would walk around a marble game, he would try to step on the nicest toy he could find. It would go up into the hole, and he would walk off with it. I know that a thief can be found most anywhere, but who would suspect a hole in the heel of a shoe to steal marbles? Well, you need to understand that a good marble shooter was generally the one with the best toy.

Let me explain toys to those of you who have never played marbles. A toy was the marble used to shoot with and needed to be just a litter bigger, a little heavier, and a little prettier than all the other marbles. Sometimes a shooter would try to use a steely, a ball out of a steel ball bearing, but for the most part, nobody was allowed to use them. At that time, most everybody had a bag or a pocket full of marbles they used in the game or to trade.

Horseshoes were another big competitive game back then. It was great to be the champion of your grade or even the whole school. The marbles and horseshoes were so popular because no uniform was required and most anybody could afford to play. A boy by the name of Clyde and I had a reputation as winners when it came to marbles and horseshoes.

The can lid war was something we were not supposed to do, but you know how boys are. It was very dangerous, and I agree now that we had no business doing such a thing. In the lunchroom, they would cut the top out of a number ten can and throw it in the dump down below the school. We would use a garbage can lid for our shield and sling the can lids at each other. It was like throwing a Frisbee, more like a saw blade but sharp as a razor. Luckily, somebody didn't get hurt really bad but just a scratch now and then.

THIRTY-ONE
Checking Rabbit Boxes

— — — — — — — — — — — — —

In the wintertime, we always set rabbit boxes to catch the wild rabbits in the wooded areas of the farm. As like most everything else we had, we built our own rabbit boxes. The best ones seemed to be the ones made of slab wood from the sawmill where the bigger pine trees had been cut from the woods.

With several boxes to check, we had to get out early in order to get the chores done and catch the school bus. It was more fun when it had snowed and we could see where the rabbits had entered the box. If the box had a rabbit in it, we reached in, grabbed the hind legs, and pulled the rabbit out of the box.

We ate some of the rabbits we caught, but we mostly sold them for a good price, fifty cents each, which gave us an idea. At fifty cents a head, if we could raise rabbits, we could really make some money. We purchased a pair of Belgium Reds and began the process of building pens. We had no idea how fast the animals multiplied, and before we knew it, we were overrun with tame rabbits. This didn't work out too well. First, the tame rabbits didn't taste as good as wild ones, and second, we had no way to market them. This plan failed, and because we had grown fond of the rabbits as pets, we had to have someone else to get rid of them for us.

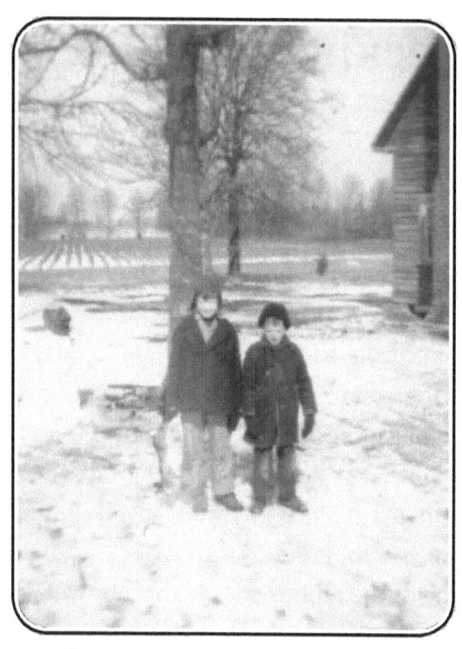

After an early morning rabbit box run

THIRTY-TWO
The Muscatine Tree

One of the favorite times of the year was when the wild grapes ripened. Native to North Carolina was one of the favored wild grapes, the Muscatine. We had a patch of woods on the farm with several small Muscatine vines, and on the back side was the best tree in the woods because it had a big grapevine in it. We could hardly wait until it was time to climb and shake the tree and retrieve those big, black, sweet Muscatine grapes. Some things stick in your mind over the years without fading at all, and that was one of them.

THIRTY-THREE

Mistletoe

— — — — — — — — — — — — —

I was thinking about the Muscatine tree and had a flashback about mistletoe. Every year when it was time to decorate for Christmas, we would take the .22-caliber rifle to the woods and shoot mistletoe out of the top of the trees. We could always get a good bunch of mistletoe from high up in the top of the Muscatine tree. Mom always liked to have mistletoe hanging around at Christmas. I would say mistletoe is probably the only parasite I liked because of the activity under the mistletoe, but even it (mistletoe) was poison.

THIRTY-FOUR

Snakes in the Henhouse

— — — — — — — — — — — — —

The flat country of North Carolina was blessed with some reptiles, some of which would do you some harm and some of which would cause you to do yourself harm.

Some folks kept black snakes around to keep down the rat population, but nobody at our house felt that way. One time, Dad shot a black snake with a shotgun and left a big hole in the floor of the granary. We came home from school one time, and Mom had stuck a pitchfork into a six-foot black snake in the chicken house. I don't know if she got that pitchfork prong in the snake by accident or if she had a good aim with the fork.

We always had laying hens so we would have plenty of eggs, and of course, snakes like eggs, too. One time, I was fairly young and not tall enough to look into the hay near the edge of the barn loft where some of the chickens liked to lay eggs so I would stand on something and reach over into the nest to get out the eggs. One day, I reached over and felt something really cold in the nest, a big, black snake. I didn't get bit, but as I said, sometimes harmless reptiles can make you hurt yourself. I was able to get away safely, but it sure could have ended painfully.

Needless to say, I never reached in a nest for eggs that I couldn't see in first.

THIRTY-FIVE
Possum Hunting

One of the things we did for fun was to go possum hunting on Friday or Saturday night.

We always had dogs but never had a trained hunting dog.

We had a place to hunt, so the dog owners found us. The guy I remember best was a Trailways bus driver whose last name was Tucker. Dad was acquainted with him because he rode the bus from Monroe to Charlotte when he was the cabinet maker at Sears. This was Dad's job for some time. He made the display cases for the store.

Tucker had a couple of possum dogs, and he would bring them down to the farm to hunt in our wooded area, which was about twelve acres. Of course, we had a flashlight or two, but the weather was generally cool and sometimes downright cold, so we carried an oil lantern to see to walk. And it was good for warming our hands when we stopped to listen to the dogs as they were running the on the trail of a possum.

We could always count on a good story about hunting from either Dad or Tucker. Tucker always had, as they say, a ball of yarn that wouldn't run out. This guy was quite a character. He had a tobacco chewing habit and always had a jaw full of chewing tobacco. This sometimes made his storytelling more interesting for some reason.

One time, my brother had come home on leave from the marines and went hunting with us that night. Now the smart thing to have with you when hunting in the flat woods, especially at night, was a compass, which we didn't have. However, Don, my brother, was a navigator on US Marine aircraft and trained to find out where he was just by looking at the stars.

After following dogs that were following the possums, we sometimes got turned around and were not sure which direction we needed to go to return home. The night my brother Don was with us was one of the nights we were turned around.

Dad said, "Well, we need to go that way, and we will come out at the end of the lane leading up to the barn."

Tucker said, "No, Fly. We need to go that way, and you are all turned around."

He pointed in another direction. My brother, who was two years older than I was, and I were too young to give our opinion as to the direction to go home so nobody asked. I really believe I could have gotten us out of there, but who knows?

Don, being the experienced navigator, went to a clearing in the woods to study the stars.

Tucker turned to Dad and asked, "Where is he going?" Dad replied," He is a navigator in the United States Marine Corp and by looking at the stars can tell us which way to go to come out at the lane leading to our barn. Tucker didn't think much of that, but said "okay" with a little laugh.

When Don returned, he said, "We need to go straight through there," pointing to a completely different direction from anyone else.

Some disagreement was expressed, but Dad finally said, "I'd say he is right." So off we went. Amazingly enough to us, we came out of the woods at the lane that led to the barn. Of course, Don was confident we would all the time.

We loved to listen to the dogs. Tucker knew his dogs and could identify them by their voice. He could also tell what they were saying. He knew if they were on a hot trail, if they had lost the trail, or if the trail was weak. Now when the dogs treed, you could really tell. Tucker would say, "Old Blue has treed. Let's go."

At that point, we would take out through the woods to find the dog trying to climb the tree. They would sometimes chew at the tree until they had a ring chewed in the bark all around the tree. Next, somebody would usually climb the tree high enough to shake the possum out of the tree. Guess who got to do that half the time?

When the possum hit the ground, the dogs were generally held back so as not to kill the possum, which they would have done if they weren't held back. The possum would make a run for it, and somebody would have to catch it and get it off the ground. If you ever saw the teeth of a possum, you would know they can have a pretty nasty bite. The idea was to pick it up by the tail and put in the tow sack or burlap bag.

During the course of the night, we would sometimes catch several possums, and they all went in the same sack. It was often my job to carry the sack, and I can remember a sack being carried over my shoulder, possums trying to climb up my back, and having to shake the back down now and then. As you could imagine, this was one of the highlights of a boy's memory.

When we had an opportunity, being the boys we were, we would gladly play a trick on each other. We used to hold back a tree branch until the next guy came in striking distance and let it go just in time to pop him upside the head. When it was a dark night, you couldn't see it coming. I don't think anybody did that to Dad.

One night, we were out in the woods, and the dogs struck a trail a good distance away so we started to try and find them.

Tucker said, "Wait. They are coming this way."

We stopped and listened for some time as the dogs came closer and closer. Finally, they were in sight, and one of them jumped up on the tree my brother was leaning up against. We shined the light up in the tree, and there it was, a big old possum.

Of course, somebody said, "Who needs a trained dog with Dick (my brother) around?"

A cat and a possum smell and sound alike to a dog, so that is what they train them with. This being the case, sometimes we would get to the tree, and the dogs had treed a cat.

A great sport, possum hunting, sure left this boy with a lot of good memories of it all, Dad, Tucker, Dick, Don, the dogs, and the possums.

THIRTY-SIX

Making Apple Butter

Many things are done while living on a farm. Some things were because most everything I know of is better prepared in small lots on a do-it-yourself basis. As far as preserving our own food, it was not only better if we did it ourselves, but it allowed us to have much more. Without money, we would have to do without whatever we wanted. Unlike today! We never thought about the poverty level, getting money from the government, or some other individual for that matter. Everyone was on his or her own to do whatever was necessary to stock up for the winter months. I am sure there were some people who didn't pay their way, but not in our family. One thing Dad taught us was to have pride and pay our own way.

One of the things we did was making and canning our own apple butter. Now Mom kept some mighty good food on the table for us, and apple butter for the biscuits she made was one of those extras. I have eaten a lot of apple butter, but none as good as Mom's. I should say we made it in an old, copper-lined iron pot. I think it was so good because it was one of the things Mom had learned to make as a young girl in the mountains of West Virginia. I don't say this just because it was my mother. She had a reputation for good apple butter, and everybody who was lucky enough to taste some of it felt the same way.

We had a few apple trees in the orchard, and when the time was right, we built a fire under the old, copper-lined iron pot once again. Of course, preparing the apples for the cooking process was a job everybody took part in. When ready, the apples were placed in the old iron pot and began the process that would result in some of the best apple butter in the world. As you might figure, this took place in the summertime, and while apple butter is cooking, it has to be stirred continuously to keep it from burning. This was a rather hot job, so Dad made a stir paddle with a handle about six or seven feet long. I can almost smell that stuff cooking right now and would pay good money for a jar of it. You may not believe it, but I was down to visit Mom one time years later and asked if she had made apple butter lately.

She said, "No, but I think there is a jar in the back of the cabinet. You can have if it is still good."

We found the quart jar and opened it. Just as I expected, it was great. After figuring out when it was made, we decided it was about eight years old. Try that for shelf life against some of the commercial canning these days.

Well, I don't know if the recipe is available or not, but I do know the copper-lined pot had something to do with the taste and color. I don't have one so I guess memories should be left alone in this case.

THIRTY-SEVEN

Fun and Games

— — — — — — — — — — — — —

As young boys on the farm, we had fun any way we could and did in several ways. Cross-country runs on Sunday afternoon was one of the things we did often, during which we ran several miles from one friend's house to another.

Horseback riding was another fun pastime. Often we were in situations where we didn't have enough horses to go round, so we ended up on a razorback mule. Riding bikes through the woods on a path we had cleared was also a great way to spend our nonworking time. With no TVs, cell phones, camcorders, cameras for that matter, car to drive, go-carts, and so forth, I'm sure you get the picture.

Another thing we did was to have dirt clod, cotton boll, and corncob fights. Corncob fights were interesting because we had plenty of cobs, and the best way to truly do a job on someone was to let the cobs soak in water for a couple days before the fight. Let me tell you. If you got hit upside the head with a soaked corncob, you knew it and made you more determined to get the guy who did it.

I got an injury from preparing for the corncob fight that left me scarred for life. Being a slender kid, a five-gallon bucket of soaked cobs was rather heavy, but if I was going to use them, I would have to get them in the barn loft some way by myself. Nobody in his right mind would help another guy with the preparation of his ammo.

I started up the ladder to the barn loft with one hand going from one step to the other and a bucket of cobs in the other hand, which, of course, was hanging below me with the weight of the soaked cobs pulling me down. Suddenly, the right hand that was going from one step to another slipped, and down I came. As I hit the bottom, I fell across the bucket on my left side. I couldn't catch my breath at all, so my brother helped me into a wagon and was pulling me toward the front of the house where my mother was.

She saw us and asked, "Is he okay?"

My brother replied, "I don't know. He hasn't caught his breath yet."

Well, that was very painful, and the pain lasted for days. Later in life, an army doctor asked about the three broken ribs on my left side. At first, I had no idea what he was talking about, and then I remembered the fall. I was scarred for life (inside).

We were playing some sort of game, and my brother was chasing me. I looked back to see how close he was, and when I came to, he was slapping me in the face saying, "Wake up!" It seems like I must have got off track just enough that, when I turned around, the trunk of a big post oak tree was in my way, and the force to my head had knocked me out. I think that was the only time anything had put my lights out, so to speak. The next time was many years later when I was in the service, but because it was another time, we won't go into that.

Riding bikes through the woods reminded me of the time I was riding rather fast, and as I jumped a log with the bike, I slipped and fell on the leaves that had built up alongside the trail. What a surprise I got as I tried to get up and get to my bike, which was lying beside the log. At first, I didn't realize the trouble I was in, and by the time I did, it was too late. Yellow jackets were going up my pant leg, and neither of us was glad the other was there. I had somehow, out of all the places to go down, fallen on a yellow jacket den, and the bike was right over the hole in the ground with yellow jackets all over it. They were working me over pretty well. Needless to say, I started coming out of my clothes, and by the time I got far enough away from the den, I was clothed only in my underwear and would have left it behind if need be. We had to wait until the next day to get the bike, so we got a rope, fastened a hook on the end, and hooked the bike so we could drag it away from the den.

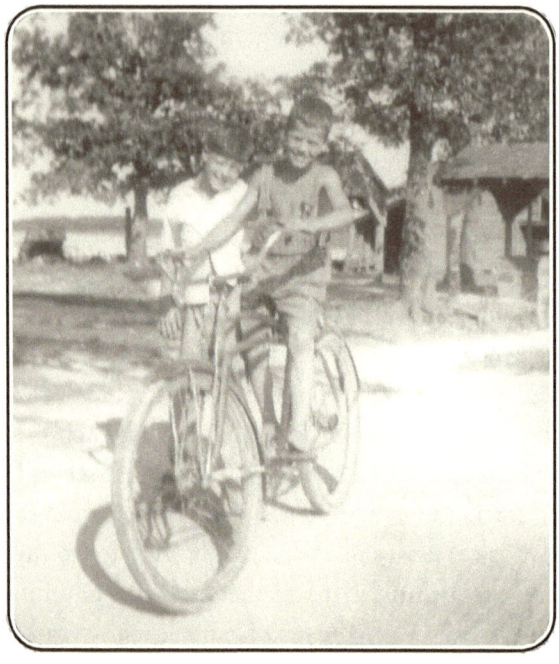

Me riding my bike

THIRTY-EIGHT

Dad and His Way of Cooking the Pig

— — — — — — — — — — — —

Warning: The first part of this story may not be for the faint of heart.

Dad knew his stuff when it came to BBQ. He loved BBQ as far back as I can remember. As I recall, when we were traveling somewhere, whether it was going to Pinehurst or Rocky Mount to see one of my aunts or the coast to fish or just on a short trip, Dad would always like to stop at a small BBQ place and order a sandwich. I think that, not only did he like BBQ really well, he also liked to see how everybody else cooked and seasoned their meat.

One of my best memories was when we would get up about four o'clock in the morning to get a fire started under the old black iron pot out in the backyard near the barn. If you have never killed, cleaned, and cooked a pig, you may not realize that the hot water was needed to clean the pig.

First, he would take one shot with the .22 rifle while the pig was still in the barn. The reason was not to stir up the pig. Doing so would affect the taste of the meat because of the way the blood system is in hogs. The bleeding of the pig was very important part of the process, and it was done before moving the pig from the farm.

Second, the pig was laid out on a pallet, and the scalding water was poured over it to make it easy to scrape off the hair, which could be done with a broken piece of glass. After all the hair was gone, the animal was hoisted up on a tripod made of three poles fastened together at the top. The art of field dressing a pig is a story within itself, so I will leave that until later. Dad was an artist with that knife and had the field dressing done in no time.

By now, the pit had been put together and was made of concrete blocks with hot coals inside it taken from the fire under the old black iron pot. By the way, fire under the pot had been burning for some time to supply the hot water used for scalding. The wood used to fire the pot was hickory, and by now, it had some good charcoal. Hickory is what we used to cook the pig because of its sweet smoke taste. Most people know that you can cook meat on various types of wood, but pork deserves hickory. In fact, even the sticks that were placed across the pit to hold up the pig while it cooked were green hickory and about one and a half inches in diameter.

Now we are talking about a pig, not a hog. This animal weighed about 125 pounds and was laid out over the hot coals in the butterfly position with all four legs cooking with the skin side down. The cooking process took about six hours with the skin side down and four or five hours with the meat side down. Dad had his own way of making sauce, and it was very good. For some reason, we never got the recipe he used. While cooking with the skin side down, Dad would take a knife and open small holes in the hams and shoulders and allow the homemade sauce smoke down in the meat.

Since this was a summertime event, it was hot, and by the time the meat could be left to cook for a while, it was nice for us boys to take off down to the pond or over to the neighbor's pond for a swim to relax and cool off.

Late in the afternoon or early evening, it was time for the pig to be taken off the pit, and I can taste it now, delicious sliced and pulled pork BBQ at its best. I have and will always be grateful to have been involved in these events.

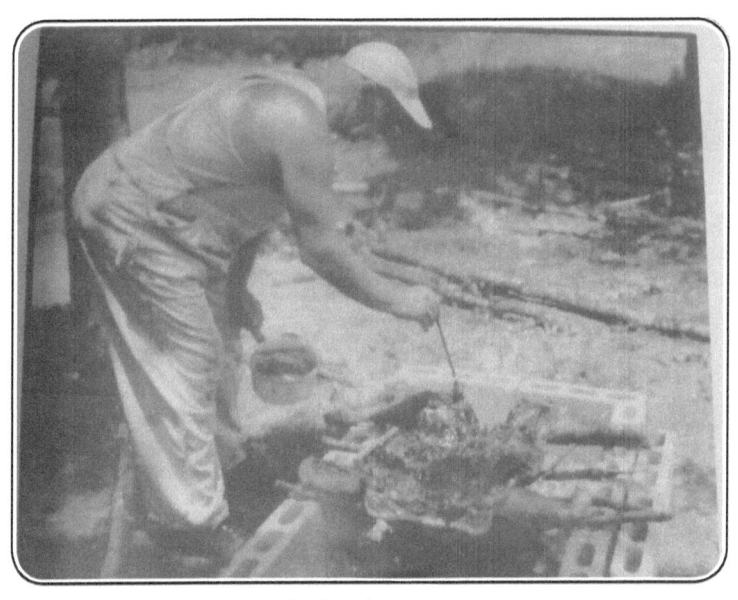

Dad cooking a pig

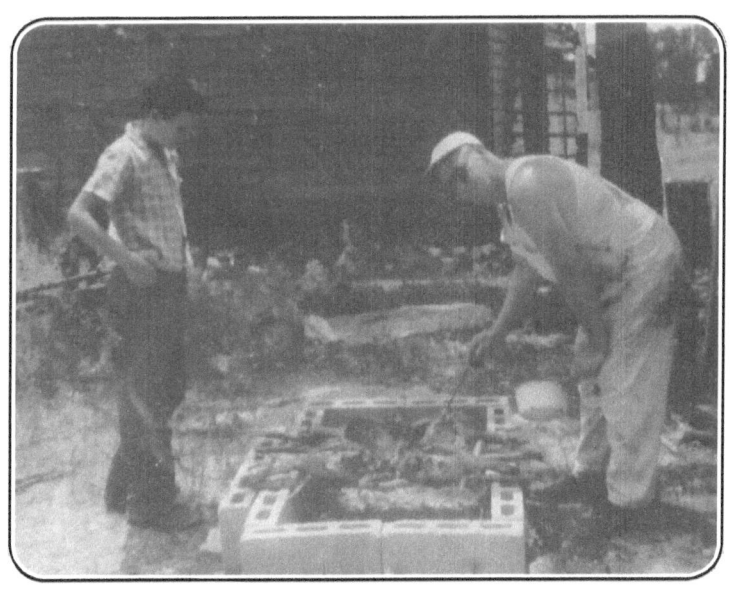

Me looking on while Dad cooks the pig

THIRTY-NINE

Exploring the Gold Mine

— — — — — — — — — — — — — —

The countryside in Piedmont, North Carolina, was made up of rolling hills, farms, wooded areas, ponds, and creeks. There was a place not too far from home that was said to be an old, burned-out gold mine with a main shaft and several levels of tunnels going out from it. In the area of the mine, there were several air shafts that went down to the tunnels so nobody was allowed in that area. However, we would get adventurous now and then and head for Howie Mine.

As I think about it today, I realize that we didn't tell anyone where we were going because we were not to be there. So if anything had happened to us, they may have never found our remains. It was quite interesting to get back in one of the tunnels in hopes of finding some real gold, but you know that never happened. I have often wondered if the mine was ever reopened, covered up, or filled in. I might even like to return and get another look inside, using a little more safety of course.

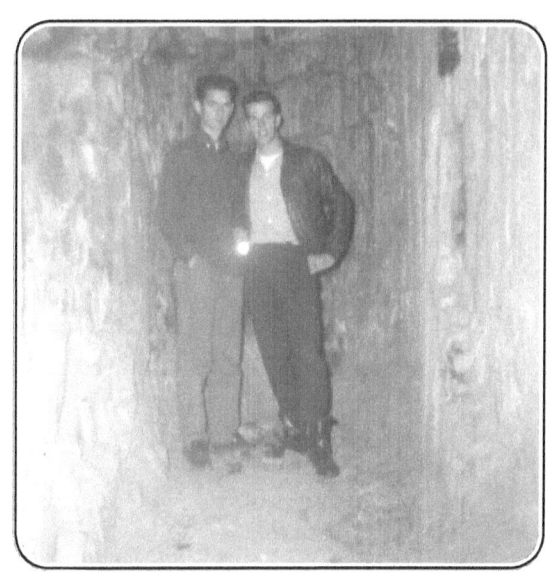

A friend and me at the end of a gold mine tunnel

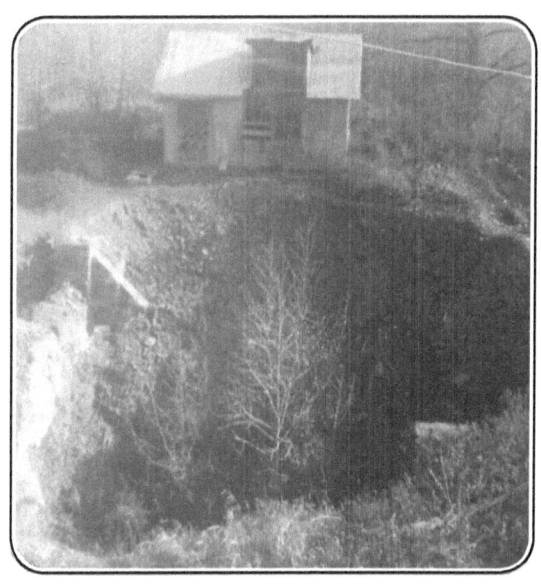

A burned-out shaft at the gold mine

FORTY

Country Cooking

My mother could flat out cook up some good country food, and she did that three times a day. Even though Mom worked in the field with us with things like hauling hay; chopping and picking cotton; gathering okra, strawberries, and corn; and doing most all the other things alongside us, including milking the cow, she also did the cooking for the rest of us. Of course, the green beans, canned corn, sweet potatoes, tomatoes, cucumber pickles, beet pickles, lima beans, fruit, and so forth were canned in glass jars (cans) and kept in the building we called the granary, which Dad had insulated and called the fruit room.

The meat was kept in the smokehouse or saltbox, and after a while, Dad rented a locker in town to keep the frozen meats, as it was mostly unheard of to have a freezer in the home. We always had a chicken in the barnyard; thus, fresh chicken for Sunday dinner was a common thing. The meal that we now call lunch was called dinner when I was a boy, and the evening meal we now call dinner was called supper. I don't know why they changed it, but I think it had something to do with people trying to be kind of fancy. Fancy wasn't necessarily something we put a lot of effort into.

One meal that Mom had a reputation for was the chicken and dumplings made from scratch. It was fit to set in front of any king. She didn't seem to mind picking and cleaning the chickens, but killing them was left for Dad or one of us boys. The story is told that nobody was around to kill the chicken one day, so she decided to do it herself. (I know that some people would wring the neck of a chicken, but we always used the chopping ax.) Well, Mom laid the chicken's head on the chopping block and took aim, but before she brought down the ax, not wanting to see the result, she turned her head. When she turned the chicken loose, it took off running as she had missed it completely. It's a wonder she didn't cut off her hand, but maybe she missed it on purpose. At least as far as I know, she never tried to kill another chicken, and the dumplings didn't have chicken in them that day.

She made dumplings quite a bit and used other things rather than chicken. Things like corn and tomatoes made a mighty good bowl of food, and she said she used those things because it made the food go further, which she needed to do with a big family.

Toll House cookies was another one of Mom's specialties, and she had a bowl of them somewhere up in one of the cabinets most of the time, but it wasn't something we just went and got as we wanted them. If we had done that, there would never have been any around. Things like lemon meringue, apple, custard, and mincemeat pie were some other goodies she made well. A snack after school for us boys was sometimes a cold biscuit and a fresh onion or tomato from the garden, which we ate like it was an apple.

Fried pork chops cut about an inch thick and that homemade gravy on mashed potatoes is something that will never leave my memory also. Dad was the kind of guy that liked fried pork chops for breakfast.

I could go on for a long time about the cooking Mom used to do, but as I talk to others, most anyone can do the same. I still feel like I was blessed to have had such good food in my growing up years—no TV dinners and no opening a can for convenience.

FORTY-ONE

Music in My Life

Music has always been important in my life, and as I recall, I was exposed to music as far back as I can remember. Dad played a guitar and a French harp along with a pair of rib bones that was used to keep time, kind of like playing the spoons as some people do today. He sang the old Jimmy Rogers-style music as we sat out on the porch in the country. There was no TV set to dominate our time. He also sang some old country and pop songs. Dad spoke and sang with a real Southern brogue and was easy to listen to.

I had four sisters, and they all sang well, but the two who came along to North Carolina in the move of 1947 were Wanda and Dorothy. When Dad would play the guitar and everybody would join in singing, it seemed to be mostly religious songs and sounded mighty pretty to a very young boy. Mom didn't sing much except in church, and that was when everybody else was singing and you could hardly hear her. I'm sure that's the way she had it planned.

One time as I remember, and I am sure it happened more than once, the neighbor kids came and brought instruments like banjo, guitar, and so forth to the house and played on the porch. I think that was mostly to be around my sisters who were in their teens, if you get my drift. Anyway, the music of those years left me with a love for music, which I still have today. That is another part of my youth for which I am grateful.

I learned to play some guitar at a young age, and when I got a chance, I would go to a friend's house, where Clyde and I or Ivan and I would play and sing country music.

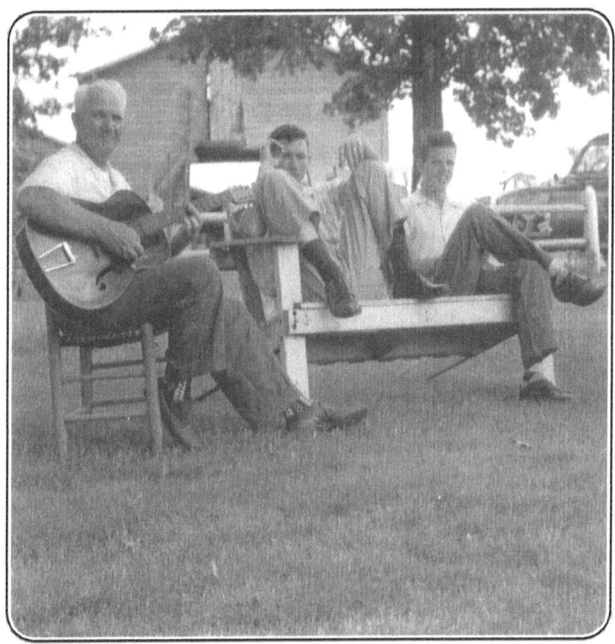

Dad playing the guitar

FORTY-TWO
Brother Goes Off to the Navy

A brother leaving for service in the United States military wasn't anything new to me, as I had a brother Edward who served in the US Navy during World War II. I was too young to remember when he joined, but I do remember when he came home after the war.

I also had a brother Donald who was drafted into the Marines and served as a navigator of a flight crew. I can't say I remember much about him leaving, but I remember well when he came home on leave, as we were all glad to see him.

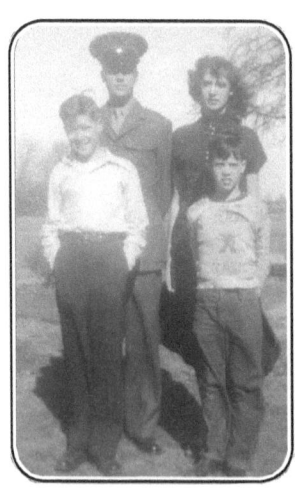

Don, home from the Marines, along with Wanda, Dick, and me

When Richard joined the navy, it was a little different because he was just a little over two years older than I was and we had spent our whole life up until this point together. He was the guy I spent time with making most all the toys, large and small, that we had to play with. Richard "Dick" did most all the farmwork we were able to do side by side with me. Dick drove the car because I wasn't old enough to drive when we had a double date.

Needless to say, his leaving for the navy was a big change in our lives. I don't think we realized how much change it was until we learned he had found his future wife in the state of Maine and would settle there and only return to the South about a year after that. It seems like that change in my life was more than any other up to that point.

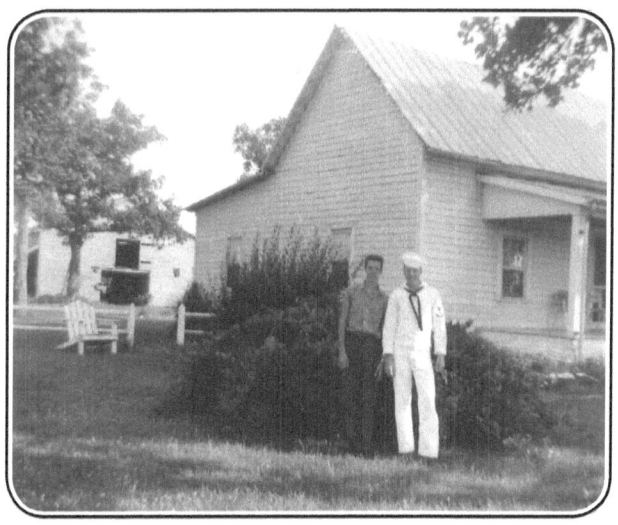

Dick, home from the navy, and me

I remember when he came home on leave. I had just graduated from high school and taken a temporary job at a shirt factory in Monroe. Since he was only going to be around for a short while, we decided it would be good if we could go up in the mountains to a place called Chimney Rock, North Carolina, and spend a day or two.

It just happened that the boss gave me a reason to quit my job, and off we went. We had a great time and spent some time at the lake nearby. We slept in the car that night. It's amazing the things that youth allows you to do without complaining of discomfort.

Military service was part of life for our family as my grandfather served in the Civil War, Dad had served in World War I, Edward served in World War II, Donald served in the Marines, and Richard served in the US Navy. And in October 1962, I joined the US Army.

FORTY-THREE

Buck, My Boxer Bulldog

— — — — — — — — — — — — —

I wrote a story about my favorite dog, Toby, and how he had to be put to sleep, but I failed to mention the dog that more or less took his place in my life. I had been fortunate to have had a dog for as long as I could remember, and not having a dog around was not a good thing. I found a young pup that I felt would meet my liking, so I brought him home and began to train him. This pup was a full-blooded boxer bulldog. I had his tail cut and his ears trimmed, which made him quite handsome. I decided on the name Buck, which he learned quickly.

Before long, Buck and I were pals, and he grew to be a stout, well-developed, muscular dog. I taught him to jump up to my chest while very young. As he got bigger, staying on my feet became a challenge for me. Knowing this, I decided that if I could direct his jump to places or people other than myself, it would be interesting, and he would improve his value as a guard dog. Buck learned to respond to my command, and with his size, he could take a rather large person to the ground if he needed to.

When I signed up for the army, I was going to have to find a place for Buck, which I approached as a serious matter. I wanted him to have a good home and, at the same time, be worth something to someone. After looking at several solutions, I finally settled on giving him to the sheriff of our county to live at the jailhouse, where he could stay inside the fence. And when I came in on leave, I could go by and see him. I did just that, and he was well taken care of and happy. I saw Buck several times after that, but I never came back to the area to live, so I never got him back.

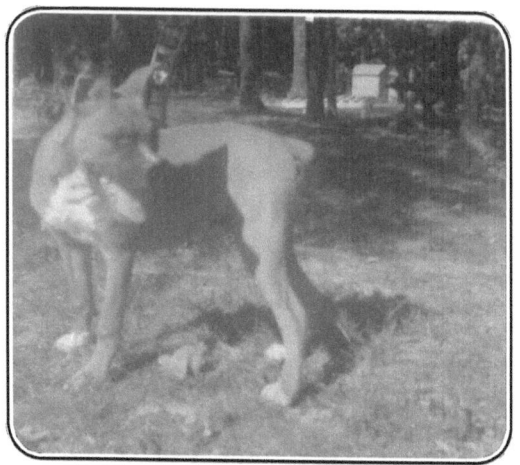

Buck, the boxer bulldog

FORTY-FOUR
Senior Play and Graduation

Unlike today's schoolkids who start planning their future career fields early, we only had a few who had decided on a career before senior year. I knew I had an interest in the electrical field, music, and carpentry, among some other things, one of which was to become a stuntman in the Western movies. I guess this interest inspired me to take a leading part in our senior play, a story about the Wild West, as Western movies were very popular in the day and most full, red-blooded young men had an interest in the cowboy way.

I was no exception, so I took the part of an old gunslinger in the show. I had been a rather reserved, conservative guy until then and had not taken part in this sort of thing, so my efforts were a surprise to many. We had a great time putting the thing together, and it went over well with everybody attending.

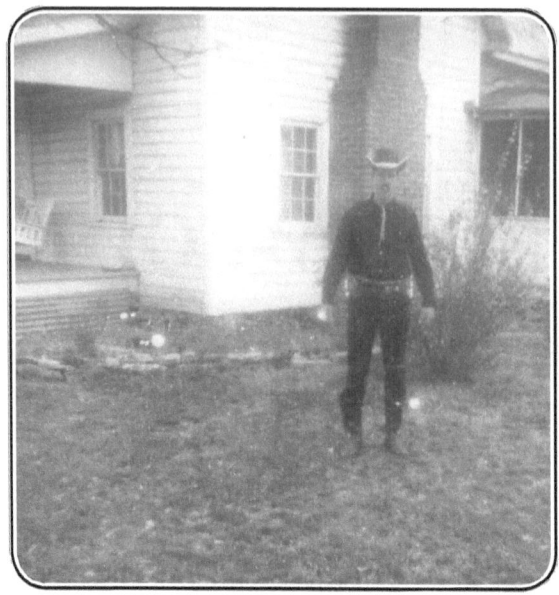

Me all dressed up for the Western play

The day came that we had all been waiting for when we walked across that stage and received the folder that contained that certificate saying we had successfully completed twelve years of formal education. With hats in the air, hugs for some, and tears for others, we were now to start the next part of life where work was the primary goal.

FORTY-FIVE

After Graduation from High School

The first full-time job I got after high school was at a place in Wingate, North Carolina, by the name of MaLeck, which was a woodshop that built decorative things from wood like corner what-not cabinets, plant holders like buckets, spinning wheels, and so forth. Leck Helms built and owned this company. He was very successful, and the products were shipped all over the country.

I was the second-shift manager and worked from three in the afternoon until eleven at night. It was a great job because I could be creative. I was never a person who felt much fear in most situations. While I was working here, my mother and dad had gone to visit family in West Virginia and left me to take care of the house while they were gone. We still lived in the country on the farm with some distance from the neighbor's house.

One night, I came home from work and arrived as usual about eleven thirty. I went on in the house and went to bed like always when the phone rang.

Someone on the other end said, "We know you are by yourself, and we are coming down."

I said, "Come on." And I hung up the phone.

The phone rang again, so I answered once more.

"We are coming to get you tonight."

Once again, I said, "I'll be waiting." And I hung up the phone.

At that point, I laid the loaded shotgun beside the bed and went to sleep.

When I woke up the next morning, I had seen no one, but for sure, someone had been there. All four tires on my car were flat because the valve stems were taken out during the night. I never did know who did it, so if it was a joke, they never got to tell it. I am glad they didn't wake me up. They saved me a couple of shotgun shells.

After a while, I took a job as an electrician's helper with a company, Steele Electric. I took this job at the minimum wage rate, which was ninety cents per hour at that time. I was making a dollar an hour at my former job, but I knew that, as an electrician's helper, I would get a pay raise in a short while, which I did. I went to night school to study electricity, and within a year, I was a lead electrician wiring houses. The last job I did for the company was a six-story grain elevator, which I was very proud of. I left this job to enter the US military in 1962.

FORTY-SIX
Just Rambling

As I think back, I never was a person during my growing up years who had to rely on the support of many other people other than family to make it through whatever I needed to do. It is evident that my best friend was my closest brother Richard (Dick), and we were together most of the time.

My sisters, Wanda and Dorothy, were in the trenches, so to speak, while working on the farm, but as most girls do, they had their minds on the boys as far as I could tell, and they were old enough to have a completely different thought process than I did. Wanda, the younger of the two, married a fellow by the name of Simon Wentz, who was a well-rounded person and could do most anything. We got along well. He had driving habits a little on the fast side, and as a boy, I thought that was cool. (Cool was not a word used in those days except for talking about the weather.) Simon had a 1957 Chevy, and as history has shown, it was one of the speedier autos on the road. As far as I know, I was about the only one he would lend his car to because he trusted my driving skills. I would use this car from time to time to take a girl out on a date. That was really going out in style. Simon became my brother-in-law and a friend.

Dorothy, the older of the two sisters, worked at Belk's department store and went to Wingate Collage, a nearby community college. We had a preacher at our church whose brother-in-law, Hoyt Rutledge, was stuck on Dorothy. After a time, they were married, and Hoyt became a minister. He also was an upstanding guy and a friend.

My brother Donald came home from the service and found a young lady named Shirley, and they were married. It was a treat when Don and Shirley would take us to the swimming pool. This pool was a not the typical pool. Rather, it was built with concrete blocks and timbers and had sand on the bottom. They played loud music that was popular during that time like "Green Door" and "Don't Let the Stars Get in Your Eyes." There were some great memories here.

I had special friends, as does everyone while growing up. Two guys in particular were Wendell Howie and Henry Underwood. Lots of time was spent with the three of us riding horses, working on cars, taking cross-country runs, and cruising town on Saturday night. After high school, we all got a job and rode to work together in Monroe, although we worked at different places. Ivan Wentz was another good friend I spent time with playing music, camping out, and picking cotton.

Not all my time was spent with the boys. I must admit I had several girlfriends and was never stuck on one girl all the way through high school. After I joined the army, I settled on one girl. This relationship was a disaster and better off forgotten. That's about all I can say about that subject. One thing for sure, it was a lesson well learned that made me a more cautious and stable person.

Following the crowd was never one of my things. When the school class went to Washington DC on the senior trip, I went to West Virginia to visit my two sisters and brother who were left behind when the move to North Carolina took place. I am sure I missed out on some things by being somewhat of a loner, but a lot was learned along the way for the same reason.

FORTY-SEVEN
The Call of Uncle Sam

As a young man, I knew, as did every young man in America, that signing up for the draft in the US military was required and had been for many years. Every young male must go to the government building and register, so when needed, the armed forces could call you into service for two years if you passed the physical examination. At that time, the draft age was eighteen years old. Knowing that several in our area had been drafted, I got word that my number was coming up and I would likely get the call soon. I decided to keep from becoming a foot soldier in a war zone. I would join the service for a three-year commitment and follow my interest in the field of electronics.

I selected the US Army to be the branch in which I would serve and proceeded with the enlistment process. On October 29, 1962, I left for my basic training at Fort Gordon, Georgia.

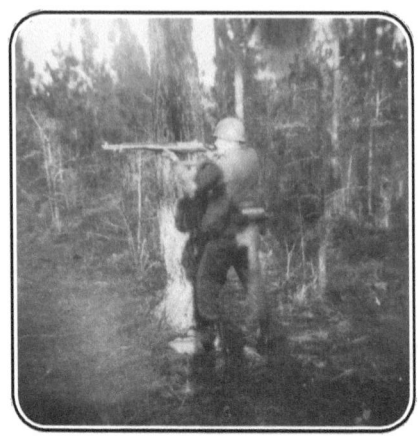

Me at Fort Gordon, Georgia, in 1962

I saw a lot of things happen in boot camp having to do with young guys from all over the country. Some of these guys had never had to do a day's work or take direction from anyone, much less take an order. These unfortunate boys had a hard time in basic because they had to conform to the regimented way of life. Some were sent home because they were unable to adjust, which I would guess saved their lives. Putting them in a combat situation would not only risk their lives but the lives of those by their side.

Due to my lifestyle and having grown up on a farm and spending some time in the public work sector, I fell into the group of guys that by no means had it easy, but we made it through the training process without many problems. At 146 pounds, I had a rather muscular frame when I entered and left boot camp at a solid weight of 172 pounds. I know you have heard all the stories about the early training programs of the army, and those of you who have served know most of these stories are true. I also believe these processes were very necessary to keep us alive in combat zones.

After graduation from basic training camp, I went on to the extended training program and became an operator and a repairman in the US Air Defense Command on the radar in the Nike Hercules missile program. With the missiles of Cuba strongly on our minds,

I was assigned to a Nike site in Deep Creek, Virginia, guarding the Norfolk Naval Air Station.

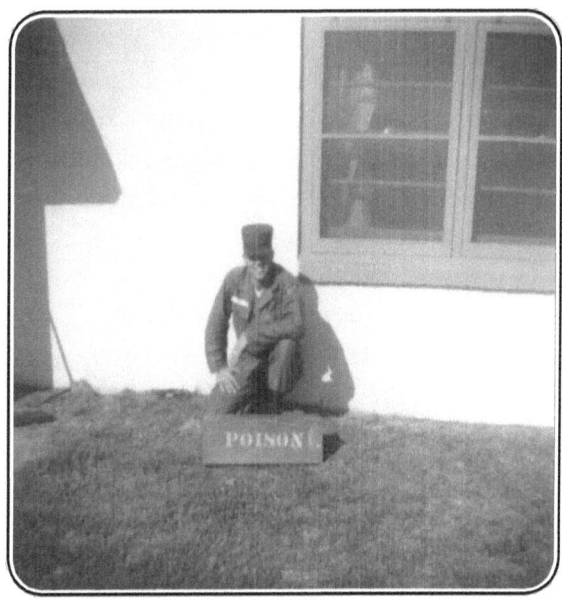

Stationed at Deep Creek, Virginia

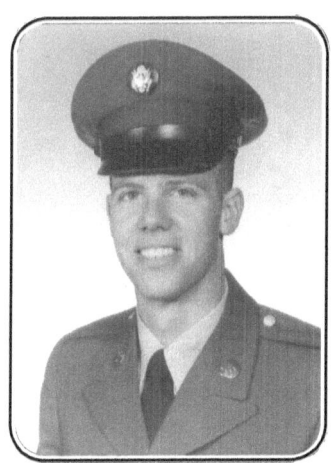

Kenneth Fly, US Army, 1962

Many things have to do with a change in a person's life, and the loss of a parent is one of them. This happened to me while I was stationed in Virginia. My dad was a victim of the mustard gas that was used while serving in the army during World War I, and as a result, he had lung problems most of his life. After being disabled for several years, he was diagnosed with emphysema with about a third of one lung capacity. He passed away at the age of sixty-five in 1963. Dad loved new things in electronics and music so we each had a reel-to-reel tape recorder and would send a tape back and forth to each other to tell what was going on in our lives at that time. The communication systems were limited in those years with no cell phones, and a regular landline phone call was always long distance, which cost too much for extended calls.

Music has always been a big part of my life, and being in the military didn't change that at all. I had my guitar and always found some guys to play a little country music with. I also played with a band of guys who were not in the military in the Norfolk area. Without the music activity in my life, I believe the time I spent in the service would have been much less to my liking.

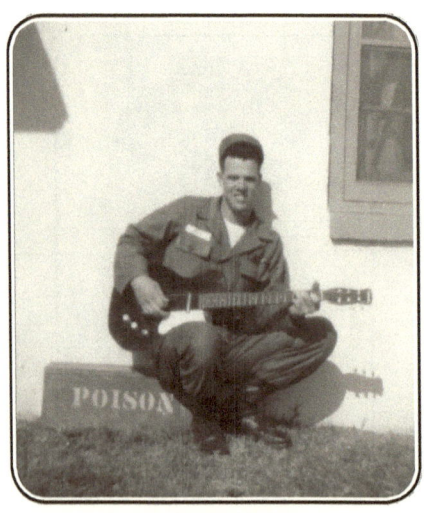

Me and my guitar

Another activity during the time I was in the Norfolk area was the purchase of a 1952 Harley-Davidson motorcycle Model 74. I spent quite a bit of my off-duty time on the bike and even strapped my guitar on my back and rode it to some music gigs. Nags Head on the outer banks of North Carolina was a place I liked ride to and ride the beautiful beaches in that area. It was an interesting experience to ride a big motorcycle onto the ferryboat from island to island as this was before the bridges were built in that area. Although I never had a problem with any other bikers, you must understand that, in 1962, the reputation of bikers had a dark side to it, and many people let you know how they felt about it, and it was mostly adverse.

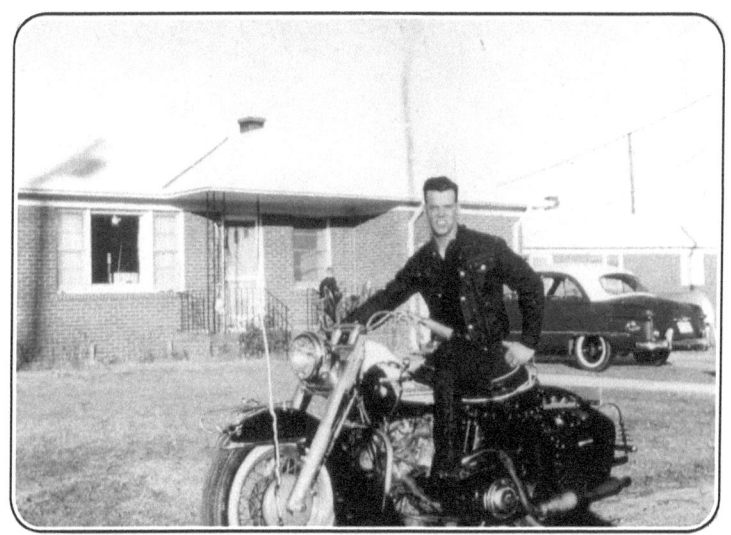

Me and my 1952 Harley in 1963

I have found that, as we go through life, things we think might amount to something positive for our future. We get caught up in things we like to do, which turns out to be good and some not so good. All in all, they come together to form our styles of life and values. One thing I always wanted to do was fly, so I allowed Uncle Sam to fund my training as a pilot of small fixed-wing aircraft. I had a lot of fun and loved being up there all alone in a plane, but it never resulted in anything of monetary value. All things considered, learning the result of a possible error was rather sobering.

After three years of service, my experience in the military was very valuable to me, and the training was the direct result of my ability to secure a job with the Erie Lackawanna Rail Road in Indiana, which launched another segment of my life.

FORTY-EIGHT
Things Have Changed

— — — — — — — — — — — — —

Many things have changed over the years, but I thought it interesting to note some of the true differences between the time I was back home on the farm and now. I think the biggest change I can see is respect. Respect for most everything has changed, but respect as related to how people feel and react to the people around them is so much different that it is hard to explain.

Some examples would be the attitude of younger people toward their elders. It was customary when speaking to an older person that you were to always use the phrase, "Yes, mama or sir," "No, mama or sir," "Thank, you, sir," and so forth. You hardly ever hear that phrase from young people anymore, and if you do, someone from my era (and generally from the Southern part of the country) has taught them. I will say, however, that these phrases are still being used by people who have been taught to be respectful to others, and it is, in my opinion, a very refreshing thing to hear.

Driving is another very vivid example of the lack of respect for others. As I remember being in town, when someone wished to enter the street, an oncoming driver would give him or her a chance to pull out while he or she gave a courtesy wave to each other as if to say, "Thank you, and you are welcome." I know that this still happens in some places, but as a rule, the oncoming driver seems to be in too much of a hurry to even look up so as not to have to acknowledge the waiting driver. Have you ever been the other guy and really needed to get out in traffic and couldn't? If so, you know what I mean. It is much nicer to visit a place where the drivers are courteous.

Then there's the subject of road rage. I don't remember that even being a problem when I was a young driver. I feel sure there was some but not like today. I guess fifty-five years does make a difference.

One of the Boy Scouts good deeds is known to be helping the older folks across the street. Well, that was just to be the way most everybody felt, Boy Scout or not. Most places you go now, if you have trouble getting around, it's your tough luck unless there is a Scout or someone from the old school, so to speak, around to help.

I guess the schools are the most changed in this subject. If a child got in trouble for disrespecting a teacher, he or she was in more trouble at home. I don't know why that has changed so much, but I guess it says their children can do no wrong. In my opinion, in that case, the parent has lost respect for his or her job as a parent, and of course, we all see the horrid results from that scenario.

What about the respect of a parent for the teachers? Wow, that sure has changed, and I will have to admit that, in some cases, the respect for the person is not due. However, if the system works correctly, that teaching spot will change, and if respect for the position is there, life will go on as it should. Whatever happened to sitting down and talking about a problem we have with someone, whether it be a teacher, parent, police officer, neighbor, and so forth. It seems like it is easier to just yell at someone about what you feel is a problem, and sometimes the person has no idea what you are ranting about.

It has been said that the best friend you can have is a person you whipped along the way. Well, I don't know about that, but I do know it will change a person's way of looking at a particular subject. For years, that has been known as an attitude adjustment, which brings me around to discipline.

I see parents and grandparents saying things like, "Stop that! Do that again and I'll whip you! Come back here now! I'm going to give you something to cry about! Don't say that again!" Sound familiar? Either kids are deaf, or they have not been taught respect because of the lack of discipline. Jimmy Dickens says it well when he said, "If you don't think discipline works, you never stole any cookies from my grandmother's cookie jar."

My brother-in-law made another rather interesting statement that I tend to agree with. He said, "A child has a nerve that runs from his ass to his brain, and if you don't hit the nerve, he doesn't get the message." Of course, there is a limit to all that.

As I grew up, it was customary for all cars, police officers, and military people to stop and stand by the car as a funeral possession would pass. Now I really didn't know, but I think this was mostly a Southern tradition because I have been several places in the Northern states where this did not happen. This act of respect may sound corny to some people, but if you are in the family car behind a hearse with the body of a family member, it sure doesn't seem corny. Fact is, it is a kind and well-accepted gesture.

We went through a time that the respect for the military people was not what it should be, but thank goodness, we are now able to thank a serviceman for his service to our country without being seen as some sort of a weird warmonger.

I have found through the years that people who have little or no respect for others are people who generally have no or little respect for themselves. I learned that respect for one's self results in kinder, more tolerant, God-fearing people, and they earn respect from others by their actions.

Many other changes have come from what is known as progress. Now there is a word that is misused many times over because it means so many different things to different people. Progress has destroyed a lot of things held dear too many people. Funny thing, many of those same people who are to benefit from change would rather whatever the change was to be left alone.

With all the change, progress, and the passing of time, I look back and realize we have adapted rather well with it all.

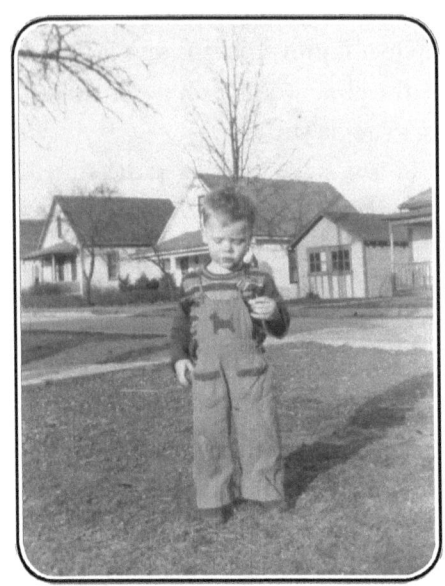

Me, age two

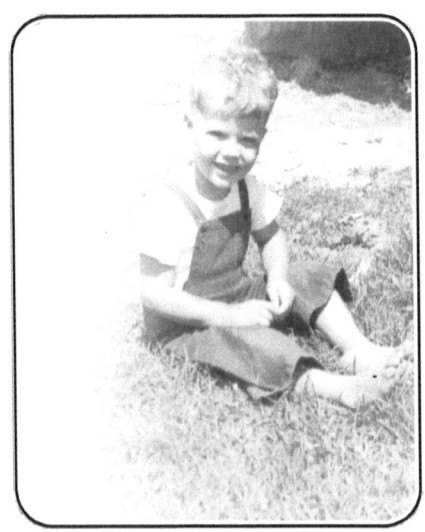

Me at age four

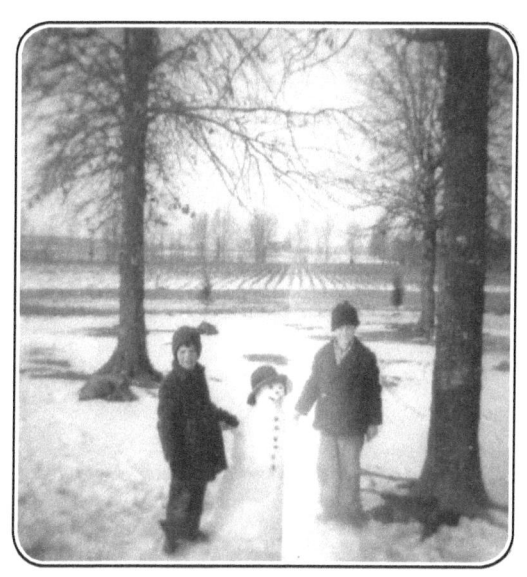

Me and Dick with snow in North Carolina

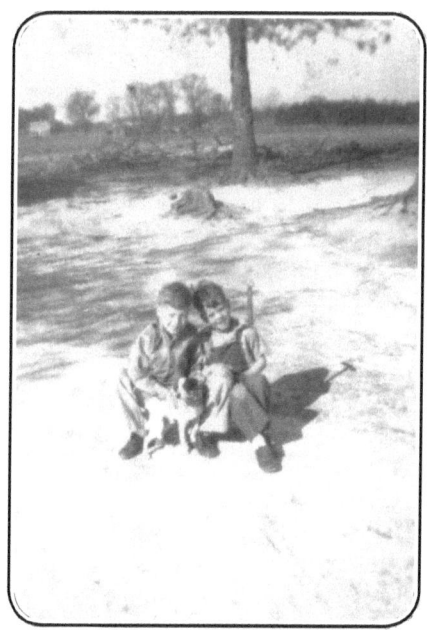

Me and Dick with Toby the pup

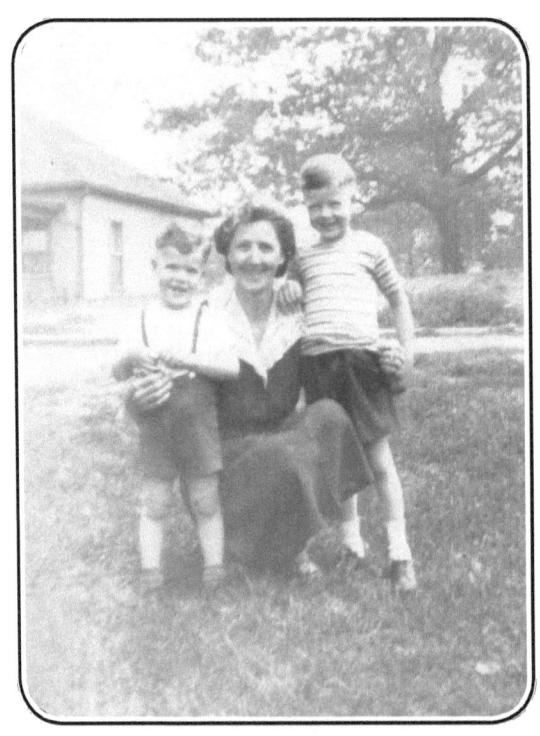

Mother, Dick, and me

DAD WAS THE HEAD
OF OUR HOME

My mind takes me back to my childhood and home
On a flat land that we owned
Where we lived as a family and upright was known
And dad was the head of our home

(ch) Dad was the head of our home
He would teach us all right from wrong
We all go through life with heartache and strife
But fall back on the teachings we've known

We can see now today many people go astray
And we hope it only last for a while
We hope they will see and return with you and me
To the teachings we knew as a child

(ch)

The time has gone by
And our childhood is gone
All over this land we did roam
But the memories are still there
With our children we will share
As we live and time will go on

MAMA FOUND A DOLLAR

December 1942, things were kinda tough
Regardless of the struggle, income not enough
To furnish gifts for all the kids, Christmas now in sight
Their disappointment would be hard to face here on Christmas night

That old Victrola horn, like a follower on a stand
Where Mom would hide a dollar so later she could spend
She had checked that old horn many times this year
She would shake it just once more for Christmastime was here

She knew there was nothing there as she turned it upside down
Something fell to the table, crumpled without a sound
Joy now overtook her as she sank into a chair
Happy kids at Christmas after all the answer to her prayer

(ch) Mama found a dollar in that old Victrola horn
A dollar, though not very much, its corners frayed and torn
Like manna from up above, it fell from that old horn
She would share it with a neighbor on this Christmas morn

Fruit and nuts was all it bought, but oh, what a Christmas treat
Gifts were nonexistent, though we had food to eat
The sharing of a dollar is all it took that year
To fill two homes with smiles and loving Christmas cheer

ABOUT THE AUTHOR

Kenneth D. Fly was born June 7, 1941, at home on Putnam Street in Parkersburg, West Virginia. He was the youngest of ten children in a family of modest means. Mother was a homemaker; Father was a carpenter with a dream of moving back to North Carolina, the state of his childhood.

Educated in public school system through high school, he expanded his education over the years to include residential and commercial electrician, US Army training as a radar operator and repairman, electronic signal maintenance on the Erie Lackawanna RR, sales and management with a multiline insurance company, Life Underwriters Training, and LUTC Fellow, Parts of CLU.

He is semiretired as a songwriter/musician and present-day restaurateur. Kenneth has enjoyed forty-six years of marriage to Samantha, whom together they have a daughter Lori, a son Jonathan, and five grandchildren.

They reside in Lynchburg, Tennessee, the location of their business, BBQ Caboose, which has become well known internationally.

www.ingramcontent.com/pod-product-compliance
Lightning Source LLC
Chambersburg PA
CBHW030811180526
45163CB00003B/1235